The Love Energy Thread

Connecting Self, Community, and Dimensions

Volume 1

SELF

By

Wendy Sloan

Copyright Page

Edited by: Sherrie Dolby
Cover Design: Wendy Sloan
ASIN: B00Q0OD36I
ISBN:13: 978-1503358959

Published in the United States by Sanhedralite Editing and Publishing

This Book is Dedicated

With Love

To the Tapestry of Our

Human Experience.

Contents

alone; there are many stepping up to the plate now and sharing the love they have for humanity and this planet Earth. We are in this together.

I started writing this book from my journals over ten years ago. You will find that I write in many voices as different aspects of my personality take the microphone. I considered editing the material for consistency, but my friends Gilda and Jean encouraged me to keep it this way because it adds character. So you will get the sense of Bossy Bertha, Toni the Tour Guide, Deidre the Soul, Adelaide the Muse, and others as you read. You never know the response you may get when finishing such a book series - where the connecting thread may take you. Perhaps we will meet someday; regardless, know the love energy thread is real and that we have the ability to feel the connection.

With love,

Wendy

Chapter 1:
Who Am I really?

Diligent in my quest

To do my best

To myself be honest

Ego mind to harness

All loving to be

Leaving me

As tranquil as the sea

We connect to Love whether we are conscious or not. I am awake to the love energy thread, are you?

We connect in our sleep.

Who am I?

What is my life purpose?

Self-Love

I was pushed down the path of conscious awareness because of pain. Not wanting to be alone the weekend after a break up, I took a workshop that was advertised in the local *Natural Awakenings*, based on Sonia Choquette's book, *Your Heart's Desire.* It was just a week before Thanksgiving of 2002. The decision to soothe my hurt, loneliness, and obsessive thoughts by doing something positive started the spool of thread rolling.

Notice how I wrote conscious awareness because we weave a patch of love energy whether we are noticing it or not.

I was no stranger to the concepts of Goal Setting. As an MBA graduate, I used the cause and effect models of getting things done to accomplish many tasks. However, this workshop inspired a refreshing shift on how I started to manifest my *Heart's Desire*. OK, I'll admit it: at that time, **ALL** I wanted to use the new insights for was to *find love,* to date, get married, and have two kids. What I've since experienced is the many ways of feeling the Love Energy connection.

To find this new great Love, I started to prepare myself and found my soulful self instead. "You need to love yourself first" was the advice most friends gave me at that time. The advice frustrated me. "But I do love myself; I am a nice trustworthy person," I would respond. I think the love yourself first line is said reactively because I was in enough pain that I'm sure I would have paid attention if the concept was explained. Problem was, I did not know who I was enough, as the soul I am. I was expecting one love relationship to give me the same feeling of connection I can now get while alone or from many sources. *I am Love.*

Another task I had written down to prepare myself for this great Love had to do with spirituality. Learning to discover your true nature of existence will provide you with a warm loving blanket of wellbeing, contentment, and happiness because you ARE LOVE, I AM LOVE, at the core of your being. Self-love starts with the awareness of your loving soul and the divine spark of All That Is Within You. Your first loyalty is to your higher self or soulful self. When this connection of love is strong, then it is easy to attract loving situations.

Journaling

One of the best ways to connect with yourself on many levels is to journal. I highly recommend you start a **new** journal as you continue on your path of loving, self-exploration, and connecting with others both physically and non-physically. You can recommit yourself to this process if this is something that you have done in the past.

If you are afraid of someone reading your most cherished thoughts, you could always burn the paper, send it out into cyberspace, or write it in your own cryptic language. And yes, I had brothers who read my locked diary as a kid, as well as a mother and ex-husband who did the same.

Do I need to sell you on the idea of journaling or am I preaching to the choir? Capture the moment, the journey of you, during this period of life as we weave the thread of connection between self, community, and dimensions. I strongly feel that you are going to have some incredible experiences as you read this book, as my clients do when we discuss these topics. You will seem to be luckier, have interesting random conversations with new people, and may have dreams to record. You may even be "activated" to be a healer or channeler as you remember who you are. Also, you may have a thought that excites you as far as a career or you may have the experience of a whole creative project downloaded to you spontaneously.

Julia Cameron, author of *The Artist Way* and *The Writing Diet,* has also seen lives transformed during her years teaching creativity workshops. She has her students write "Morning Pages" to unblock creativity and noticed over the course of her twelve week program that many students lost weight and transformed in other aspects of their lives, too.

Journaling is my number one recommendation along the Path of Self Exploration because it is a tool to connect with many aspects of self. Some parts may need healing and mental reframing. And the writing has a way of attracting to you what you love, need, and want.

Self-Exploration

So what do I mean by Self-Exploration? Learning about yourself is a lifelong process because the persona of yourself changes with interactions that you experience. We are imprinted by our primary caretakers while growing up and are socialized how to behave in groups like school and work. However, the effects of conditioning are altered when we expand our experiences.

Personal transformation is not a destination of achievement but a continual process. So the question is, how can I simulate / stimulate your self-exploration when it is such a personal task and this is a book not a personal interactive session? Stories, illustrations, ideas from other authors, and writing assignments will provide a template for self-exploration. Be aware and journal about the advice you give to other people; it may be more for you. ☺

What has been your pattern or template of living? The image of Leonardo da Vinci's, *Vitruvian Man*, comes to mind as a good example of physical proportions and symmetry which also represents the geometric design of the whole universe. ***You could stop here and journal about your physical life history noticing any patterns, themes, or resolved issues.*** The personal coaching field uses the phrase:

"Let go of what no longer serves you". Sometimes, our patterns and issues come up again so that another layer of the onion can be peeled away.

We are like a Swiss Army knife with many hidden attachments. We know that each tool is there to use, as needed, providing a sense of security that allows us to maneuver life with confidence. The woman who performed my first aura chart told me I was expanding my beliefs and learning to use tools and resources that I forgot I had, so it is more than likely that I am not going to tell you something that you do not already know, but I may refresh your memory to the great everlasting soul that you are. Thus, as I hand you "Love Energy Glasses," connect the thread by writing in your journal.

Exercise: What did you notice about yourself this week? What makes you feel good? What question is most important for you to get an answer to? What are you most curious about learning about yourself?

Science of Cells

As a massage therapist, I have witnessed how cell memory is triggered by touch and as a hypnotist, I have observed how repressed memories create templates of energy that run emotions and behaviors. Learning how we work and how to uncover and shift limiting thoughts is a worthwhile skill on our Self-Love path. As a channeler, I can tell you how overjoyed souls are when clients learn how to lead with the true loving astute essence of who they are and no longer let their ego run the show.

Energy is stored in your cells. Because the energy is alive and present now, we can think of these threads as active, and they weave in the present what was active in the past and created in the future. You could say that there is a DNA strand that is your past lives. We are *All That We Are* and we are connected to *All That Is.* There are some great books on quantum physics to explain the science of this. You could say part of the cell's energy is alternate lives or dimensions.

The first time that I had my blood analyzed, I was amazed at the picture under the microscope. Just one drop looked like the starry universe. It looked like a *National Geographic* picture of the Milky Way. I felt a strong connection to everything and heard an inner voice that said, *"Pay attention here- we are one, this is how it works."* I then saw a flash of that popular picture of the tree with roots that says, *As above, so below*, in my mind's eye.

Cell memory can be triggered by all of our senses. The scent of vanilla, pine cones, or sautéed onions and garlic can bring us to such a memory. A song on the radio can remind us of the time you first heard it played and all that you were doing in your life at that time. Emotions may flood your being when viewing old photos from your childhood.

Mindful Energy

Learning how we work is going to be helpful on so many levels. Our culture sure could do a better job in educating our young people on how the mind functions. There is more to the inner workings of the mind than just learning about the brain. We now know that vital chemicals carry messages between our brain, cells, and muscles. The process is hidden from our view but the energy of thoughts affects how we feel and is vital to our health and wellbeing.

Ann Wise, author of *The High-Performance Mind,* has researched what the brainwave states of beta, alpha, theta, and delta do and how they work together to provide self-healing, solve emotional problems, improve relationships, and promote better general health, relaxation, and stress management.

Some of my clients need assistance in guiding themselves into a state of stillness. They always use the radio, TV, and electronic games to keep their minds busy. It is as if their own inner anxiety prevents them from being alone. Pay attention to your thoughts and do not let the internal "itty bitty shitty committee" get too loud.

"You need to learn how to select your thoughts just the same way you select your clothes every day. This is a power you can

cultivate. If you want to control things in your life so bad, work on the mind. That's the only thing you should be trying to control." — Elizabeth Gilbert, *Eat, Pray, Love*

Astutely focusing on the way we do want our life to be helps to counter balance other influences that might not have our best interests in mind. Advertisers pay millions and billions of dollars to control your mind and wallet by linking their product with images of happy families and parties with attractive friends. They don't link their beer with a panhandling person outside a convenience store or their fast food with an obese customer struggling to fit into a booth. TV flicker rates are designed to bring your brain waves into the Alpha brainwave state so that you are more open to suggestion. Be aware that it may not be the product you want but the feeling of love, popularity, and connection the product "brings" with it.

Mirrors for Each Other

Our mind and feelings are the love energy thread that connects self, communities, and dimensions. We may love to spend time by ourselves reading, journaling, and walking in nature. However, we can learn a lot about ourselves when we interact with others. Do we seem to take on the same role in most of our relationships? Do we assume the same energy dynamics? If we were an actor or actress would we be type-cast? Do you like how you get along with other people?

Our reactions to people we first meet can be intense. This cell memory gives us the opportunity to connect more consciously. Embrace what feels good and release the need to be dragged into a drama that can be avoided even if it feels familiar. Emotions are a gauge of our thoughts and beliefs about our circumstances. Just as pain tells us something is physically wrong, uncomfortable feelings can be the sign that change is needed.

In December of 2002, I saw a flyer advertising a "Soul Mating and Dating Workshop" to be held in Deerfield, Florida. I took the flyer and got directions to Jack's home. The teacher, Jack, and his friend Bob were all that showed up that night, so the discussion we had was very informal. Bob was an astrologer and made the comment that there are only two

15

emotions: LOVE and FEAR. I had to question him about anger, and he explained that anger is the result of fear: fear of loss of respect, fear of not being heard, etc. He further stated that when you want to do something and you hear a small voice that tries to stop you from doing something fun, you should question yourself to see where the decision is coming from: love and excitement or fear. He also talked about this intriguing town, Cassadaga, near Orlando. My own Google search had me strolling down the streets of this Spiritualist town and buying my first pendulum within the month.

Who are your friends? Have you met some new people and collected a few new business cards? Perhaps you should make that call and set up a time to meet. New friends are like flowers that need sunlight-energy, water-activity, soil- time, and time to blossom. Care for your new seeds today with a contact.

Meeting Sally

It was February of 2003, while sitting at Jack's Reiki circle waiting for it to start when he told me about a reading he had just gotten from a gifted medium who was a channeler. He said I had to meet her and invited me to a presentation she was giving the following week. For a second, I felt fear come up because of past religious teachings, but I quickly told myself that I could just meet him there and if it was too creepy I could just leave and never do it again.

This "Otherside Chat" was held in a New Age book store. I did take my own car and was pleasantly surprised how tranquil the energy felt in the room. Candles were lit on the covered table, where a sign was displayed, **"Energy is Everything."** *'Wow,'* I thought, *'That is so true; the saying is so concise and true.'*

I took Sally Baldwin's card and called her within the week. Over the course of many years, I had private sessions with her and took classes. Sometimes we even traded services and I, along with Rose Hunt, helped edit her second book *Otherworldly Answers To Earthly Questions*. She peacefully transitioned in her sleep the year that I lived in California in 2012. When I returned to Florida, I resumed my friendships with the spiritual support group that she had founded.

Looking back on those first readings, I am surprised how readily I accepted the new ideas that resonated deep within me. Sally was a great spiritual counselor who was patient and kind as I explored and tried to piece together new concepts. I was an avid new age reader at that time and would come to her with new ideas and people to channel. What I enjoyed the most was the way Spirit expanded upon my reasoning, cautioning while it was true, as far as it goes, to be careful about the terms we use and how once we label something it becomes a *thing* with an energy all of its own.

The Love Energy Thread has a way of putting people in your path at the right time to support you, and the reverse is true, too: you are there to spur others on their path. Be willing to share and accept new invitations. Do not let fear stop you from seemingly random opportunities. The exchange of energy may be more impactful and meaningful than what was already scheduled on your calendar.

Soul Charts

Like Sally, the first time I meet with a new client, I prepare a soul chart to discuss the template of energy that is imprinted when they are born. The chart is a tool to use that is very eye opening. You could compare it to an Astrology or Enneagram chart. This way of looking at yourself is helpful so that you can understand how to allow the flow of love energy from your essence be front and center in your life, without letting the body / mind / ego run the show.

Back in the 1970s, a group of friends that lived around Berkley, California met to connect with Spirit and were given a body of information from an entity that called itself Michael. The Michael Entity is a group of 1,050 souls who once were in human form and who now teach from what is called the causal plane or dimension. They have empathy for those in physical bodies and so have the ability to communicate and translate information that is helpful.

Some of us come to the Earth more often than others and so we are more comfortable being in human form. We come for a **cycle** of lives and our strongest imprint is the **role** we use for the entire cycle. Then, for this lifetime, we have a **goal** and **mode** of being with an **attitude**. We are also imprinted from our parents or caretakers with a **chief**

feature, which is like an obstacle to overcome, that manifests after the age of twelve. We **center** ourselves intellectually, emotionally, or moving and also have a **body type** influenced by the planets. (Note: the words in bold are better defined in the Appendix.)

The true purpose of introspection tools is open to greater love and understanding of our physicality and to then have compassion for others. Most times when we have misunderstandings with others it is because one or the other of us, or both, are coming from the more ego aspects of our personalities. Awareness of our own proclivities can help with communication and learning how to bring out the loving soul energy effectively.

I have the Soul Overleaf form and charts in the Appendix. This is good for those of you who are already proficient in using a pendulum. A book on the Michael Teachings will get you started or you can contact me for a reading. This is not a shameless plug but a sincere offer to help you with self-discovery.

The Collective, The One, The Tao, Jehovah

All cultures have their own language and expression of the God energy. Who we are in relationship to the greater presence is the topic of many books, poems, and art. Some people like to talk about the higher self or the I AM. **There is something about the words, I AM, that puts forth a sense that you are part of it. How can you even speak the words I AM and not envisioning yourself as part of it?**

That is where so many in the earth plane, in the world of the human being, find themselves cut off from the most wondrous and energetic force of all. They see themselves outside of Jehovah, outside of God, outside of the strongest, most lovingly astute energetic field or force that exists. Then, of course, that sets up all kinds of weird and recriminating situations on the Earth. That, of course, then begins to build strength as it is given attention and energy.

You cannot exist without the astral while in human form because it is there that you have the sense, the greatest and most wondrousness of the I AM presence, of the recognition of God, the One, Jehovah, the Almighty, Yahweh. The dream and trance state allows the human mind to take a back seat to the feeling and knowing of oneness. We are more connected than our culture teaches and many, even

21

old, souls have an attitude that they can't wait to die and go home.

There is a shift happening to such a degree that it is being felt; a sense of recognizing the fullness and the wonder of what the human experience really is. Jill Bolte Taylor, in her book, *My Stoke of Insight,* describes her stoke experience of **Oneness** in detail. There are others who have written about their near death experience and/or hallucinogenic trips that describe the pulsating love energy field. Just looking at an Alex Grey painting gives you a whoosh of visual connection.

We really can't separate out the God in us, but we can feel a separation when the mind has no sense of purpose or our beliefs see us as separate. Gregg Braden has written the about the science of our cells in *The God Code* and also concurs, like myself, that if more people understood the universal nature of humanity, we could resolve deadly conflict. How can we exist happy, as the grand souls we are, in a culture that is slowly shifting alongside those who are resisting change?

Human Needs, Wants, and Desires

"Know thy self and to thine own self be true" was advice given from father to son in William Shakespeare's play *Hamlet*. Being clear about your heart's desire and bringing your thoughts and feelings into alignment with your hoped for experience attracts it to you. Sometimes there is a time lag in physicality and sometimes you get something so close that you change your mind and start putting energy into another desire.

Let's face it: many of us just feel better when our perceived basic human needs and wants are taken care of. There is some truth to Maslow's Hierarchy of Human Needs chart. However, does happiness depend on stuff? No, idealistically it shouldn't, but the extra stress and energy to balance yourself into a state of peace takes a lot of energy, too. The Buddha says that all suffering is caused by desiring; however, our souls came into physicality to experience what it is like to be here in the culture and place of our birth.

We are all individual as to what our set point is of abundance and lack. Broke to one may mean scaling back on the number of days for an expensive vacation and to another lack is making the choice between using the last ten dollars for gas or food. Honoring our egos' reasonable desires is natural. Sometimes we need to reign in the thoughts of desire so that frustration does not set in. Even in times of lack, allowing our minds to speak hopeful thoughts will allow the powerful chemicals, which we naturally produce, flow to give us a sense of well-being.

There may be many things we desire, but there is one thing that we need: **The Astute Loving Energy Connection** simply expressed as these Four Astute Aspects: **Love, Support, Excitement, and Humor.**

This is a good place to stop and journal a few words about this topic. Where do you choose to put your energy? What do you desire? Do you need help or guidance?

Going Within

To find and feel the Love Energy Thread is an easy thing to do. Just putting your hand on your heart, closing your eyes, and deep breathing can start the process. This technique has the benefit of slowing your brain waves and heart rate. Using your imagination, thinking about a beautiful place in nature, and saying soothing words like I AM peace, I AM calm, can shift your energy and restore balance. Just be willing to let go of outside influences and thoughts.

Eric Butterworth, author of *Discover the Power Within You*, explains that Jesus understood the Kingdom of God was within and this knowing was the theme of his ministry. I'm sure someone has counted how many times Jesus said "Fear Not" and "The kingdom of God is within your midst."

There is wisdom beyond our consciousness when we go to this quiet place in the mind. The wise man or wise woman inside, the depth of our soul, can communicate when we push the ego aside. Great ideas come to us when the mind is still. Spontaneous thoughts may come to you in the shower or doing yoga. Journaling may start to feel like automatic writing after a couple of pages. Huge benefits come to those who find their own way of going within.

Burning Nag Champa incense is my personal ritual when I am committed to going within. I encourage you to find your own techniques and tools to help you do the same. Perhaps lighting candles or listening to soothing music will help you. I had one roommate who would chant to reach this place within. The rosary was created to be such a tool. The prayer state is one of supplication and receiving of guidance. Don't get bogged down with the terminology; find the Loving Voice within.

Guided meditation recordings may be useful to some if you are visually inclined. Books may catch your eye, at the right time, to answer a question. Classes and people we meet may be a direct answer to complement our practice of going within. Getting confirmation about the validity of our inner thoughts along the way fuels the strength of our loving connections. Acknowledging the synchronicity of events brings more opportunities for the same. You just feel luckier and more part of everything that **IS.**

How Do You Connect and Learn?

How we consciously connect to the Love Energy Thread is individualistic. Trying to connect in the same way as another can be frustrating. For example, I was exasperated with the early meditation and past life regression CDs I bought. Or shall I say I was down on myself and thought something was wrong with me because I couldn't see the blue sky and green grass. I have also met many people who think they can't be hypnotized because they were told to sit back in the audience after volunteering to participate in a hypnosis show. Stage hypnotists are skilled at picking people that go very deep, very quickly for entertainment purposes. Not everyone gets to trance and meditation states by visualization.

With clients, I do a few warm up exercises before trance induction to see how visual they are. I simply ask them to close their eyes and pretend to see a bird or flower. About 80% of the clients are able to see the image; some see it quickly and then it fades. The other 20% process information by a combination of hearing, knowing, or, as they describe, *"I just made it up."* Knowing how they process information is helpful going forward to clue me into which types of words to use and also to make them confident of their abilities. I ask them to just go with it or change my words in their minds if I use a seeing word when they are not visual. I give them permission to sense, imagine, or just make it up. This way, the mind can slow down and go easier into alpha and theta brainwave states.

The Neuro-linguistic Programming (NLP) classification of learning channels are: Visual, Auditory, Kinesthetic, and Auditory Digital (which I think of as Concept). NLP states that 90% of all communication problems are because people are using different channels. Visual learners process by seeing pictures. They will look up to visualize and recall events or even close their eyes to picture what they have learned in their heads. They draw pictures to help remember and to map out driving directions. Auditory learners store information by the way it sounds and have an easier time understanding spoken instructions than written ones. They may need to speak the written word to know it. The eyes move side to side as if to hear the information they wish to recall. Kinesthetic learners need to touch and do "hands on activities." They tend to look down to remember how something made them feel. If you are a tactile learner, you may have difficulty sitting still. Auditory Digital learners get their knowing all at once and may need time to explain why they know what they know. They link one concept to another and "get it" quickly. Do you see yourself here? What is your expanding style?

Dying to Live Again

Many of our decisions in life are influenced by our fears, being obsessed about security because the thought of dying brings a feeling of anxiety. We, as a culture, have sanctified life at all costs and as a result have actually made it harder for some souls to stay. This is why illness and the resulting change of routine sometimes give souls a chance to find pockets of astute loving energy that then allows them to stay in physicality.

The change in lifestyle, search for healing practitioners, and a dropping of some of the restrictions, responsibilities, and practices that seem to be required to fit into our culture are socially excused due to the illness and process of getting well. Like the Phoenix rising from the ashes, some experience a profound sense of renewal. Perhaps some of you reading this book have personally transformed because of such an experience. You did not have to die and review your life to shift into an expanded version of yourself. Maybe you even had a **Walk-in** or **Braiding** experience that really has shifted your core essence.

When souls are ready to leave the earth plane, they benefit from our acknowledgement and acceptance of the impending transition. We give this on a subconscious and soulful level whether we are aware of it or not. Several hospice nurses I have met agree that the families can do much to ease the letting go process. Death bed experiences of being in both worlds before the last breath is common.

Most people do feel, see, or hear dead loved ones. I ask clients, "Did you see, feel, or dream about the person after they died?" The most common response is, "Yes, I still talk to her all the time; I know my mother is with me now." I quite often get a rush of energy on my right side, my hairs stand up, and I get goose bumps when I ask such questions. I've learned to take this as a conformation for me and a sign of connection from the Otherside. *What mystical experiences have you had that give you the knowing that there is more to life than just our physical bodies? How does this influence your decisions and behavior? You can write about this in your journal and don't be too surprised if you find yourself sharing the story soon.*

Creating a Personal Philosophy

All of your experiences, knowledge, and conversations with others are like patches of energy. Weaving and organizing these into a beautiful quilt is what having a personal philosophy is all about. Writing this book has been that for me, an answer to the challenge of, "If you don't believe in our way, then what do you believe?"

I'm not saying that everyone needs to be so formal about their ideas and produce something as tangible as a book. There is no need to be vocal or preach to others, although by your happiness and ease of living you may be asked what makes you tic. The replacement of thoughts and attitudes that do not serve allows the flow of love energy to affect your being and be noticed because when you let something hang on longer than where you are, then it becomes the thing that drags you down. Be rid of it and allow the metamorphosis.

Happiness is not a single destination but a feeling which flows inside. *Be open to the flow of energy that is so astute, so full of All That Is, that you are immediately and continually recognizing your oneness. That is what all souls are seeking. The doing part comes in with the physicality that you are part of and that, of course, is understood. But it must not be mistaken with the goal, for the purpose, or the reason for existence. It is simply a matter of who you are in this plane, in this moment, in this aspect of yourself. That is what you must come to remember and to allow yourself to realize is what dictates how your experience in the earth plane prevails.*

The soulful part of us sees the big picture, the whole quilt of experience. There are many colors and textures of thread which we, in this lifetime, have access to weave and play with. Consequently, we have a wonderful opportunity in this lifetime to choose thoughts and actions that promote love and a sense of connection. *Focusing attention on the feeling of what we want and taking action on our inner wisdom bring excitement and a sense of hope. Finding gratitude and humor in our present situation allows us to feel the peace and wonder in the moment. Just breathe: take a big breath and release it slowly.*

Chapter 2:

Healing the Present, Past, and Future

No problem can be solved from the same level of consciousness that created it.

-Albert Einstein

Many times before a person can feel the depth of the Love Energy Thread, some healing and reframing of events needs to take place. Making peace with where we are in our current situation and focusing our attention on the positive can bring a sense of gratitude. We don't have the luxury of a negative thought when we are in crisis because the vibration of fear and anxiety are counterproductive to Love. My basic recipe for healing and happiness is:

60% action towards how we want life to be, job, friends, positive attitude, hopeful

20% uncovering of the past, reframing events, making restitution, reflection

20% skill building for the future, planning, taking classes, visualizing future events

The recipe is tweaked depending on your individual present circumstances. Seek first to understand, balance and imagine all possibilities. I think of what I was taught in Kindergarten here when we were taught fire safety: **To Stop, Drop, and Roll.** Good advice in any crisis.

Stopping to feel good in the present changes your energy field. Start rolling down the path towards physical healing. *Healing is not about the result per se but the process of feeling the thread that connects one to source energy. The moment brings everything to you, even if the physical results lag.*

The Now

I want you to think of this page when you are in the need of some inspiration because the NOW is the most important concept to understand and feel the Love Energy in the present: to feel love, excitement, hope, and a general sense of well-being. Balancing Tools: Having a self-care kit already to go like a parent with a diaper bag or a traveler with a carry-on bag. What do you have NOW?

Deep Breathing	Aromatherapy	Take a Nap	Meditate
Read	Draw	Listen to Music	Call a Friend
Reiki	Go in Nature	Take a Bath	Journal
Exercise	Drink Water	Crafts	Self-Hypnosis
Yoga	Hit a Pillow	Take a Drive	Ride your Bike
Go do Errands	Pull Angel Cards	Cook Something	Say a Mantra

What makes you happy? List 3 things you do that make you feel joyous:

1.

2.

3.

How do you balance yourself quickly? We all have seasons of discontent but after we wallow in the mud, for however long we choose, it is so nice to know we have the skills to easily get out of the pit and take in a shower of happiness.

Accept where you are NOW; past choices and decisions brought you to this current point. We can support our own unique evolutionary healing and spiritual process more easily with an attitude of peace and hope. We want to be still enough to hear our own wise inner voice. Have faith that you will be guided to the right information, place or person.

Who's Your Healer?

Today, most people take a proactive role in their health care by learning as much as they can about their treatment options. Each person is theoretically responsible for his or her own health, but this line gets blurred when physicians and insurance companies get involved with managing care. Keeping the immune system healthy by eating nutritious foods that keep the body alkaline is beneficial. A lifestyle that includes exercise, yoga, and massage will reduce stress and illness.

There are many caring and skilled doctors but most did not get much education on nutrition, medicinal herbs, or the importance of the lymph system. Their instruction has been skewed by the alliance of universities and hospitals with the pharmaceutical companies. Healthy living makes more sense than having to risk the high rate of medical errors found in hospitals. You are ultimately responsible for your own health.

Diane Stein, author of *All Women Are Healers*, gives the history of how the past, peaceful, Goddess honoring civilizations were slowly and sometimes violently overtaken by nomadic tribes of patriarchal people with weapons and chariots. Women who were trained in the healing arts were the ones who cared for their villages until the burnings of the

Inquisition. Wealthy families sent their sons to study in church-sponsored colleges, and laws were passed that required degrees and licenses to practice medicine.

Today, in my state of Florida, there are statutes that give only licensed medical and mental health practitioners the right to "diagnosis and cure disease." It is legally necessary for alternative practitioners to get written referrals from licensed medical professionals and inform the public their protocol, "is not intended to diagnose, treat, cure, or prevent any disease." However, many hospitals now have added these effective complimentary therapies to their menu.

How quickly clients recover may depend if there is a hidden reason to stay sick (secondary gain). For instance, if a woman gets better she will no longer qualify for disability and need to provide for herself. The illness then has a reason for continuing. Patients involved in a lawsuit want to feel better but to get a settlement they have to show the severity or permanence of the injury.

Modalities of Healing

Medical / Mental Health	Nutrition	Hypnosis
Exercise / Yoga	Massage Therapy	Acupuncture
Chiropractic Care	Reiki and Energy Devices	Herbs and Aromatherapy
Stones and Crystals	Affirmations and Humor	Time / Acceptance

There is no one template to healing that works for everyone every time. The unexplainable we call miracles. Josh Rosenthal, author of *Integrative Nutrition,* uses the word biodiversity when referring to the fact that not one diet is perfect for everyone. To determine which healing modality is right in the NOW, you will need to tune into your body responses. Declare you will heal and find an answer. There is so much more to what is transpiring on the energetic levels and fields than have been even discovered or bandied about in the scientific community.

Food is our best medicine. Nutritional eating is a matter of quality and quantity. Our diets should be rich in vitamins, minerals, enzymes, and antioxidants. Alkaline foods are best. Choosing fresh, whole, unprocessed foods are better for us. Make sure that the nutrients are not wasted by overcooking or the use of the microwave. Allergies can be noticed when we pay attention to how our foods make us feel. Genetically modified fruits and vegetables have caused severe reactions and even death to unsuspecting consumers. Even though our food supply has been tainted by a company's desire for profits, there are super foods like coconut oil, moringa, turmeric, curcumin, and many others that provide help.

In spite of our best efforts to practice good wellness habits, we can compromise our immune defenses by chronic stress and exposure to toxic chemical pollutants. Getting the right amount of sleep is important, as is moving the lymph system for detoxification. A complete exercise program includes aerobic activity, flexibility exercise, and strength training for optimal physical and emotional wellness.

Massage therapy is great for relieving stress and improving circulation by bringing oxygen and other nutrients to body tissues. It relieves muscle tension and pain, increases flexibility and mobility, and helps clear lactic acid and other waste from the cells. Swedish massage is the most common form of massage therapy in the United States. Therapists use massage oil or lotion on the skin with long smooth strokes, kneading and using friction, focusing on the muscles.

Therapeutic-grade essential oils and blends are formulated to support the body's own natural ability to keep itself healthy and can be used in a diffuser, applied on the skin, or ingested. They can be effectively used in combination with traditional medical practices. I had a personal experience of the superior effects of a eucalyptus blend that was kindly given to me for a lingering cough. After two unsuccessful prescriptions, it was this aromatherapy that got rid of my chest cold and cough that I had had for over three months in just two days.

The plant kingdom has medicinal and vibrational healing properties which bring forth relief to the human condition. Most people do not recognize the full value of them because the synthetically produced pharmaceuticals get more attention. This does not mean that they are more effective. In every area of the world, there are plants which provide healing, balance, and the wondrous sensation of love. Many healing plants grow without any cultivation efforts and have been used for eons by those who recognize their effects. Animals in the wild instinctively eat what their body needs. Informed self-care may first have you making a medicinal tea before reaching for an over-the-counter drug or prescription.

Stones and Crystals each have unique healing vibrations. Elixirs can be made by putting washed stones in water and setting them outside to catch the sun's rays. I was substitute teaching at an Elementary school when one of the mothers came in to show the children all the different kinds of crystals and stones she had. I had had an argument with my boyfriend before the start of work and was still feeling upset, running the conversation over in my mind. I asked her which stone was best to relieve stress. She handed me a black, white, and grey stone called Snowflake Obsidian and I immediately felt a wave of calm come over my body. She had my attention. *Love is in the Earth* by Melody was my first book about the properties of crystals and now I have *The Crystal Bible* by Judy Hall sitting on my shelf. You may find the stones will talk to you if you let them. ☺

Healing is About Connecting to the Love Energy

When we tap into that love that is so divine, we have no idea what we are doing in the physical. So often it's that stuck place of being separate, distinct, and different that we play out in our lives that causes the health problems we experience. People want to understand and then find a cause and effect cure to implement but our soulful, esoteric self would prefer to just experience the subtler energy fields of whatever modality or healer joins with us. It is all about loving so look for a practitioner who gives off the attitude that you are me and I am you, we are in this together. There are few opportunities in our culture that allows this, but healing offers both parties the platform, the opportunity, to extend – to find the connection and to feel it in every way possible without expectation of a result.

One of my massage clients invited me to experience an energy machine called the QXCI. It was a fascinating computer program that worked on the subtle quantum energy field. When I researched further, I was surprised to find that in the 1930s, Raymond Royal Rife invented a machine which he called a Frequency Instrument. He succeeded in curing cancer, but his work was suppressed by a powerful smear campaign and conspiracy headed by the American Medical Association.

Today, the term quantum healing is used to describe a process whereby a person's health "imbalance" is corrected by the quantum field. Different disciplines use this phrase and use their own protocols to do the shifting. Deepak Chopra integrates the Ayurveda Indian system of medicine with quantum mechanics, Dolores Cannon's Quantum Healing Hypnosis Therapy technique involves inducing a trance to question the subconscious mind and provide a quantum healing, Vianna Stibal teaches her students to go into a trance to provide a Theta Healing, and Richard Bartlett's Matrix Energetics method uses students' creative power to time travel and transform issues by fundamental quantum physics.

With total recognition and acceptance that the love energy thread is there for you to experience in a variety of ways, you can go forward with no need to demonstrate illness in such a physical way. This is not to say that one has the excuse then to go down a path that would be unhealthy or destructive. Do not exercise any intention of that nature. You realize that you are a being, total and complete, just not fully understood or comprehended; realizing with no need to fill there is no need to fix. Just be healing in the NOW, so that health can happen.

Personal Way of Healing

It all goes back to the intention. It all goes back to joining in out of love. Having faith that you will attract what you need in the present moment to balance yourself. And even if what you need seems to be out of your grasp, you do have the ability to use your creative imagination to have it now or shift the need for it in the first place. The experience here on earth is multi-faceted and is not just what it seems to be on the surface.

You will have to decide what is best for yourself, but I am willing to share how I keep myself healthy. I don't smoke and back in 2002, a random comment in Doreen Virtue's book, *The Lightworker's Way*, struck a chord within me when she said that she found not drinking alcohol increased her psychic abilities. When I feel a cold coming on, I cut down on activities and get more rest. I eat healthier, use aromatherapy, and monitor my stresses. For aches and pains, I will use peppermint oil and perhaps get a massage. If the discomfort lasts, I will see an acupuncturist or chiropractor depending on the issue. I also use self-hypnosis to see what thoughts and emotions are influencing me. I also like to see what Louise Hay's, *Heal Your Life,* books says about my issue, so I can meditate on a positive affirmation. I may do some Reiki on myself and use Dale Olson's book, *The Pendulum*

Chart's vol.1. Then, I may play with some crystals and pull a few oracle cards or I might read a book and take a nap. Chapter 4 of *Kryon Book 6* also comments on integrating modalities.

It is so much easier to take care of yourself while you are well to avoid sickness than it is to make a comeback. It is more fun to meet people and trade services to experience those subtle loving energy fields and modalities than having to be a patient. Last October, I slipped on some water at a store and fell flat on my right hip and hurt my left arm that protected my head from the ground. I managed my own care by cranial release technique massage, orthopedic doctor for an x-ray, chiropractic adjustments, laser light therapy, and lots of self-healing with Reiki, peppermint oil, and Jacuzzi time. I didn't see clients for two months as I recovered giving my body the time it needed to heal

Not all illness has a physical origin like my fall. The autonomic nervous system, DNA, energetic influences of our emotions and stress are not observable but through trance states we can explore, study, and shift what is hidden.

When and Why Did the Illness Start?

The seeds of disease are planted before the first symptoms appear and way before a full blown episode. The cause could be part genetic, rooted in childhood trauma, or part of past life baggage. Feeling overwhelmingly sad, guilty, or blaming yourself is not helpful. Remember the 60/20/20 happiness recipe? We will balance ourselves in the present, put on our detective hat to get clues from the past, and use our imaginations to create a healthy future.

But first, is this illness part of the soul's plan to exit this earth? I have asked people straight out, "Do you want to get better or do you feel it is your time to go?" The bluntness of the question opens an important dialog about their wishes, expectations, and desires. Knowing the mental state and what they are telling themselves about leaving is so important. The first time I did this, the words just flew out of my mouth spontaneously. I was asked to do some energy work on a woman because she was suffering from multiple issues. Her life force was so low, I wondered if I was being called to help her heal or to help her pass. Her eyes told me she just then decided to stay when she answered my question.

Another question to ask in the case of a serious illness is, "Do you believe in miracles?" Yes and, "Do you believe you are worthy to be healed?" If not, why not? If you received a healing today then how long would it take for you to see the physical results of this healing? This is important for some clients to believe: yes they are healed, but it will take "X" amount of time until they can fully recover.

I was asked by an acquaintance to go to her mom's house to do a massage, and I said NO, her mom would need to come to me if she wanted me to help her. After I got off the phone I thought it was weird that I had refused to go to the woman's house. I felt that if she truly wanted a healing, she could make the effort to come to my business. I questioned the knee jerk response of my ego by channeling the mom's soul and got an interesting message. It seems her mom was ready to leave the earth plane soon and that my service to her was to just acknowledge that the soul was ready to go. She did die within the month. In this case, the reason she got ill was to provide a path to leaving.

Learned Behavior Patterns

Our parents and caretakers out of good intention try their best to impart their wisdom onto us so that we can fit into the society into which we are born. This process of both learning and teaching is how our way of life continues. Emotional reactions are also learned ways of behaving. Ask any kindergarten or elementary school teacher and they will remind you that children must be socialized to conform to such things as sitting in a seat, raising their hands, and walking in a line

According to psychoanalyst Alfred Adler, our birth order predicts our personality. First-borns are natural-born leaders who feel responsible for those around them. Middle children are typically the mediators and peacemakers. The youngest are the more playful and develop a sense of humor to get attention. The only child has characteristics of both oldest and youngest. They are also thought to be precocious and prefer adult company and conversations.

Gender socialization is the process of learning the social expectations and attitudes associated with one's sex. For example, girls and boys may learn to do different household chores. Sometimes gender roles and expectations lead to inequality and restriction. Helplessness and courage are also learned as a child grows to find the amount of influence they control. Experiences of abandonment and fears of the dark all have an energetic thread that can be mitigated.

It is common sense that if you give someone a reward for doing something, they are more likely to do it and if you punish them for doing something, they are less likely to do it. Our food preferences have been shaped by our upbringing and sometimes given as treats for good behavior. Religion, spirituality, and how we feel about people of other cultures are all learned and taught to us when we are impressionable.

Bruce Lipton, author of *The Biology of Belief*, says that as children we operate mostly in theta brain wave state and so form perceptions and beliefs about life years before we acquire the ability for critical thinking. The good news is that we can NOW choose what feels most loving and astute. *Is there a long held belief you want to journal about to challenge, change, or experiment with?*

The Birthing Experience

Based on my clients' experience while regressing them, I can tell you the fetus does recall the events before birth, although there is not one universal template for the time that the soul and consciousness fuse with the body. Some souls linger around a woman before she gets pregnant and so can recall events before the development of the body. The subconscious mind of the fetus also records all of the experiences while in the mother's womb and also receives the thoughts and feelings of the mother as its own. The fetus can see, hear, experience, taste, learn, and feel while in the mother's womb.

Many emotional and physical problems, such as feelings of loss, rejection, separation anxiety, panic attacks, depression, headaches, and sinus problems, can be traced back to the traumas surrounding birth. The trip down the birth canal involves a series of twists and turns relying on the uterine surges to propel the child forward, the **pulling** from external forces can cause strain patterns to the body tissues and craniosacral system, instilling a feeling of being rushed. Whereas a delivery by C-section could implant a lifelong feeling of, "I can't do it by myself, I always need help."

There has been more than one hypnosis client that has had the thought, "Why am I coming here again?" while riding down the birth canal. It is difficult for some souls to bridge the gap – to feel as if they can be the soul they are in such a dense and physical place of existence. So many want to feel it, so many want to experience it and yet so many find themselves so covered up, so densely burdened by that which is of the physical that they cannot get through it and feel the wonder of the physical and feel the excitement of being here knowing they are the souls they are.

The birthing process can be gentler. Marie Mongan, author of *HypnoBirthing the Mongan Method,* believes that every woman has within her the power to call upon her natural instincts to bring about the best possible birthing for her baby and herself. The bonding between mother and child, or lack of, colors the thread of intimacy for the young infant. How needs were met and if they were done in a timely fashion affects our disposition and frustration levels as adults. *What was your birth story? Did your mom and you have an easy pregnancy? Journal now about the earliest memory you have.*

Sexual Exploitation

Healing from sexual exploitation is individualistic. You could reason the mind's ability to disassociate and forget is an act of love. However the vague feeling that something is not right or that something has been forgotten haunts a person so as adults, clients are ready to look at events from childhood. Damaging emotional imprinting comes from feelings of powerlessness, fear and, shame; however, some of the most scaring effects come from the aware caretakers that did not believe, protect, or stop the situation but rather condoned or encouraged the exploitation. What the child told himself or herself about the experience is most revealing to help the adult unravel stuck energy and heal.

To find emotional closure on some event in your life, Dr. Phil McGraw recommends that you identify and execute your Minimal Effective Response, the least thing that you can do that allows you to get emotional closure. I use this idea with my hypnosis clients, asking the subconscious mind what it needs to do to feel better. Surprisingly, the response can be very simplistic but always individualistic. Forgiveness is a choice, a choice that you can make to be free from the emotional threads that bind you to an event not of your choosing.

Carolyn Myss, author of *Why People Don't Heal And How They Can,* cautions people from remaining in support groups past their shelf life of use. Groups can provide vital initial assistance and insight. Having sympathetic, nonjudgmental, and dedicated support to explore feelings and to be heard is helpful but because the underlying criterion for remaining a member of a program is to accept the group's hidden message, "You will always be a victim" it leaves people wearing their deepest wounds on their sleeve like a red badge of courage. Refusing to let go of events robs your energy in the present and can then deplete your body of vital energy to remain healthy.

Past exploitations can be healed and the way paved for new compassionate interaction with others. A new story can be told of how the small acorn becomes a powerful oak tree. Energy integration is saying, **"Yes, this happened to me, but this event or period of my life does not define who I am."** Suppressed emotions and memories are at the root cause of many addictions.

Addictions

We all have a certain level of anxiety; it has been a part of the human collective conscious for eons, and it takes effort for most to transcend this energy. The reason that a substance is sought is because it makes the brain produce chemicals which soothe our mind. We want that trance-like feeling of love and home, so it is with good intentions, to feel good, that a substance becomes a crutch.

This is more about recognizing that love is replaced, as you know quite clearly in the physical, with whatever brings about a comfort level. The sensation of connection and knowingness when one is in the substance - in union with it if you will – having the experience of total and complete bliss. This is what draws souls to this kind of substance and why it is so difficult for them to extricate themselves. It brings such wonder, a sense of peace that they do not have in their, perhaps, non-addictive state. When the addiction brings forth that sense of peace or bliss, it is not with an awareness of knowing that. It is almost a separation out – "I feel myself, I know myself to be at peace and, perhaps, in some loving state, but I am not connected. I do not feel my connection to others and I do not care to."

There is so much judgment and fear of relapse that produces its own energy of anxiety for the addicted and those who love them. It is as if somehow you instill more fear in the one who is attempting to become non-addicted. Of course, this is an anxiety-comfort cycle that will just simply continue until the awareness matches the recognition that there is something about the experience that is bringing that deeper sense of love. Getting rid of that need for comfort, and the satisfaction coming from the illusion of what the mind and ego creates, helps. Once knowing this truth, you can begin to feel the love energy affecting you more, and you can realize that instead of reaching for that old worn out pattern of use, you are truly and completely willing and able to give up the old way for something you do not know or understand. You are willing to step into a void, being willing to be in the **now**. Another way to assist this letting go, if the mind must know, is through a regression session to decode the subconscious source of anxiety and reframe any past trauma.

Energy Threads from Past Life Experiences

When a client in a trance is asked to go back to the first time they experienced a certain emotion, most of the time they go back to an event from this lifetime but sometimes they go back to a past life type experience even if they don't believe in that sort of thing. Modern-day researcher Dr. Ian Stevenson has identified over 3,000 cases of children who remembered having been someone else in another lifetime. Carol Bowman in her book, *Children's Past Lives,* describes how her hypnotist house guest solved the mystery of her five year old son's sudden hysterical fear of loud noises. With his eyes closed, her son described being a civil war soldier, shot in the right wrist, bandaged up, and ordered to return to battle. He reluctantly returned to operate a cannon, not wanting to be there. After this short impromptu session, the fear of loud noises disappeared and the eczema on his right wrist vanished completely, and it has never returned.

What was said at the time of death from the last life can also be an energy imprint that affects this lifetime. One client died in a prison in South America and vowed never to live there again and so she carried a lingering fear of traveling south. Another client's anxiety was the result of her last lifetime's avenged death for locking people in a building and setting it ablaze. When and why do past life experiences get triggered? I'm not sure, so it's a good thing a client's subconscious mind can untangle the issue. The pattern I do see is that when similar emotion or situations are felt at the same age, the bleed thru effect is more common. For instance, the woman who was out of work and seeing her savings being depleted with the physician's diagnosis of psycho-somatic neck pain coincided with regressing to the time of the French Revolution and being fearful of being beheaded.

Simple phrases while in a trance such as, "That was then; this is now" or, "Now that you are completely free of _____ you are able to _____," work to shift the lingering, stuck energies. Simply commanding the divine love energy to effect a change and then imagine witnessing the change take place does the healing, too. Ask the higher self for advice or experience being attended to in a crystal healing room. Imagine going before a high council and pledging acts of atonement. You can watch a new contract being signed, debt being repaid, scales of balance being restored. Some sessions may require post hypnotic action or ritual to complete healing the past. What is really meant by healing the past is to change the effect of the past and bring about a brighter future by acceptance, energy integration, and mental reframing. This healing frees the mind and allows the energy to flow.

Self-Forgiveness for Future Happiness

Are you ready for a fresh start? Let's put all the "shoulda couldas" behind us and move forward with love. Self-forgiveness is all about undergoing a change in feelings and attitude about an incident. Change the story. Thinking an act was unforgivable may be motivated by love so we don't do it again, but it can cut us off from the love we are. Shame affects our self-worth, and guilt may be more about the consequences of getting caught, not what we did. Healthy remorse will cause you to acknowledge the capacity for causing harm as well as your potential for doing good.

Forgiving yourself may be most beneficial when you feel like you deserve it. What can you do to make it right? Is some sort of restitution needed or will a heartfelt apology clear the air? Ask what the other person wants in order to make it right. They may offer an idea you had not thought of to balance the harm. Perhaps time needs to pass before your apology is accepted. Then it is up to the other person to decide if they forgive you. Receiving forgiveness from others can help facilitate self-forgiveness, but it's ultimately up to you to decide when you've done enough to right a wrong. It may be useful to consider what kinds of reparative behaviors will actually make a difference for others or for your own personal growth. Self-decided punishment should be mild and time limited and never physically or psychologically harmful.

What is there to forgive from the soul level? When I channel souls, they admit on the physical level they were flawed when alive but make no apology for the energy they are at the core. Many times they joke about the personality of the past and silly things they did. Becoming aware of our proclivities and taking steps to live in harmony with our environment protects us from stress and anxiety. Having lived thru difficulties gives us compassion for others.

We did hop around to many ideas and concepts in this chapter and that was done on purpose because there is not only one linear way to heal. Getting out of our own way allows the physical body to feel the divine love energy which is our true north and heals the present, past, and future with a higher level of consciousness.

Chapter 3:

From Thinking to Feeling

People are just as happy as they make up their minds to be.

- Abraham Lincoln

Growing up, my dad would often tell us kids that if "you want to be enthusiastic, you have to act enthusiastic." However, my mother would get irritated at my ability to laugh and joke at negative situations. She often said, "Wendy, not everything is so funny." Now, as an adult, I can use discernment in serious situations; however, one-liners still do fly out of my mouth. Depending on the company, I may just say I was channeling George Carlin. ☺

Sometimes as a kid, I would feel confused or stressed when I was logically told to act or feel a certain way because that was what God wanted me to do, even when I felt something else. I was told that the heart could not be trusted, and it was better to trust the wisdom of *The Bible*. It is ironic to say that the company I now keep reminds me to get out of my head and go into my heart. Stop thinking so much. My friend Gilda gave me a clear, cracked crystal to sit and meditate with to feel more. There was unexpressed anger, jealousy, and sadness still hidden.

Hearing my own inner voice has helped to clarify and shift hidden emotions, the ones you don't want to express for fear of criticism. This chapter begins by discussing beliefs and religious convictions. Next, we will explore how the love energy of the heart can provide emotional opportunities. Further, we will delve into how the dark night of the soul is a season to feel the hidden aspects of self. Lastly, we will discover how the intertwined nature of the soul and ego is felt as we make decisions without being stubbornly willful. Fear takes a back seat to the exciting and loving possibilities that we can create.

Beliefs

How do most people develop their beliefs?

Parents and care takers	Teachers and Classmates
Religious Teachings	TV and Media
Friends and Workmates	Personal Reading and Experience

What are Memes?

Memes are ideas or paradigms that are commonly held in cultures. Memes are to ideas as genes are to bodies. They replicate like a joke, theory, or urban legend. Some are helpful and some take us down a path that is non-astute. Some memes seem neutral and other's negative implications are not felt until centuries later. For example: "Become fruitful and many and subdue the Earth." "Stay in your marriage at all costs, for the children's sake." "A company's primary responsibility is profits for the shareholders." "We are God's chosen people." "We must stop the infidels." Memes and beliefs can be conscious or hidden in the subconscious mind. These thought forms can be changed and do evolve over time, sometimes to more helpful ideas but often they try to keep the status quo. This word was coined by Richard Dawkins in the book *Selfish Gene* as a concept to explain the spread of ideas and cultural phenomena. Sally was the first person that I recalled using the concept, and she directed me to a wonderful book called *Beyond Civilization* by Daniel Quinn. Many today are challenging the ideas of our culture because our current trajectory does not seem sustainable or much fun.

Challenge why you believe what you do, experiment with new experiences, and see for yourself how you feel. If a teaching does not resonate with you, test the validity of it. Understand why it is taught and under what circumstances it still seems relevant. It was 1993 when I made a decision to get out from the religious conditioning I was under. I had to figure out who I was and what did I believe. I found I am love and loved because I AM not because I Believe.

Religious Convictions

Have you notice how emotional and passionate people become when talking about their religious beliefs? Commonality of beliefs can bring a strong sense of connection and community. Many enjoy loving fellowship with people of the same faith. Some groups are more tolerant then others and most are willing to live neighborly with people of another faith. So much unease in individuals, communities, and in nations comes because we put too much meaning to the words in holy books and try to follow them intellectually instead of with our heart and inner knowing.

The Pew Forum on Religion & Public Life's new 2014 survey details 28% of American adults have left the faith in which they were raised in favor of another religion or no religion at all. If change in affiliation from one type of Protestantism to another is included, 44% of adults have either switched religious affiliation, moved from being unaffiliated with any religion to being affiliated with a particular faith, or dropped any connection to a specific tradition altogether. Most people keep the faith of their families but changing is not so unique anymore.

After reading many new age books and seeing the similarities to some scripture, I asked myself if there was an author who blended the wisdom of both. Within a week of asking that question, I was given a small book by Yogananda from a friend who was moving out of state. He did connect the similarities between both worlds and so I then bought his *Autobiography of a Yogi,* which I found much more interesting than memorizing all of the muscles for my massage anatomy test. Months later, I read about Madame Blavatsky and the Theosophical Society. There are many interpretations to the same words.

Elaine Pagels' books examine early Christian texts and question the wisdom of religious orthodoxy as divinely revealed truth when the writings were founded in a society espousing contradictory viewpoints. As a movement, Christianity and Gnosticism were not coherent, and there were several areas of disagreement among the different factions. Gnosticism attracted more women because it allowed female participation in sacred rites, like the faith of the Essenes. No wonder Constantine formed the Council of Nicaea in 325 a.d. to attain consensus in the church through an assembly of bishops representing all of Christendom who were known for both fostering love and for divisiveness.

Issues about the divinity of Jesus and cannon law were debated.

The resulting centuries of edicts stand in comparison to the simplicity of the two simple commandments, "Thou shalt love the Lord thy God with all thy heart, and with all thy soul, and with all thy mind", and "Thou shalt love thy neighbor as thyself." Have these statements influenced your life?

We also have anti-religionists who, like Carl Marx and Vladimir Lenin, see religion as the cause of suffering and feel it is the opium of the people. Spiritual oppression is where the masses are working for an ideal future better life in heaven, while allowing their present to be exploited by beliefs that keep them isolated and impotent. They are taught to be submissive and patient while those who live off the labor of others are taught by religion to practice charity to the less fortunate to gain entrance to heaven. Religion has been a sort of spiritual booze in which people drown their human potential. Modern banking money systems and the suppression of our connectedness to other realms are being controlled by these institutions. History has shown us that religious institutions have attracted both the loving and kind and those who love power and control.

Back in the 1970s, there were a few TV evangelists who were exposed for fraud and for sex scandals. The Academy Award for Best Documentary Feature in 1972 went to *Marjoe,* a film about a child preacher who was taught by his parents to perform "miracles" and receive large amounts of monetary donations, even though he had no personal faith. After suffering a crisis of conscience, he invited a film crew to accompany him on a final preaching tour to show how evangelists manipulate their audiences. Regardless of the hidden agenda of these ministers, I remember parishioners, little old ladies standing behind their pastor saying, "But he healed me! I used to walk with a cane and now I am free of it!" Faith and the mind even with a religious placebo can and does heal. Something is going on here that is important to notice: seems as you believe, so it is.

Years ago, I was introduced to a group of people that studied a book called *Urantia.* There is something of a mystery surrounding the authorship and compilation of the book, but the energy contained within gives illumination, a sense of brotherhood and connection to all that is. The book is broken into four sections and the first two sections are quite intellectually dense. The third section is about the history of earth, Urantia. The last section is about Jesus: the religion of Jesus not the religion about him. My biggest take-away from this book that I have picked through is Jesus' Talk to Nathaniel which exposes the **meme of the infallibility of the scriptures.** I want to share this entire perspective. *Urantia Book* paper 159 chapter 4:

159:4.1 And then went Jesus over to Abila, where Nathaniel and his associates labored. Nathaniel was much bothered by some of Jesus' pronouncements which seemed to detract from the authority of the recognized Hebrew scriptures. Accordingly, on this night, after the usual period of questions and answers, Nathaniel took Jesus away from the others and asked: "Master, could you trust me to know the truth about the Scriptures? I observe that you teach us only a portion of the sacred writings — the best as I view it — and I infer that you reject the teachings of the rabbis to the effect that the words of the law are the very words of God, having been with God in heaven even before the times of Abraham and Moses. What is the truth about the Scriptures?" When Jesus heard the question of his bewildered apostle, he answered:

159:4.2 "Nathaniel, you have rightly judged; I do not regard the Scriptures as do the rabbis. I will talk with you about this matter on condition that you do not relate these things to your brethren, who are not all prepared to receive this teaching. The words of the law of Moses and the teachings of the Scriptures were not in existence before Abraham. Only in recent times have the Scriptures been gathered together as we now have them. While they contain the best of the higher thoughts and longings of the Jewish people, they also contain much that is far from being representative of the character and teachings of the Father in heaven; wherefore must I choose from among the better teachings those truths which are to be gleaned for the gospel of the kingdom."

159:4.3 "These writings are the work of men, some of them holy men, others not so holy. The teachings of these books represent the

69

views and extent of enlightenment of the times in which they had their origin. As a revelation of truth, the last are more dependable than the first. The Scriptures are faulty and altogether human in origin, but mistake not, they do constitute the best collection of religious wisdom and spiritual truth to be found in all the world at this time."

159:4.4 "Many of these books were not written by the persons whose names they bear, but that in no way detracts from the value of the truths which they contain. If the story of Jonah should not be a fact, even if Jonah had never lived, still would the profound truth of this narrative, the love of God for Nineveh and the so-called heathen, be none the less precious in the eyes of all those who love their fellow men. The Scriptures are sacred because they present the thoughts and acts of men who were searching for God, and who in these writings left on record their highest concepts of righteousness, truth, and holiness. The Scriptures contain much that is true, very much, but in the light of your present teaching, you know that these writings also contain much that is misrepresentative of the Father in heaven, the loving God I have come to reveal to all the worlds."

159:4.5 "Nathaniel, never permit yourself for one moment to believe the Scripture records which tell you that the God of love directed your forefathers to go forth in battle to slay all their enemies — men, women, and children. Such records are the words of men, not very holy men, and they are not the word of God. The Scriptures always have, and always will, reflect the intellectual, moral, and spiritual status of those who create them. Have you not noted that the concepts of Yahweh grow in beauty and glory as the prophets make their records from Samuel to Isaiah? And you should remember that the Scriptures are intended for religious instruction and spiritual guidance. They are not the works of either historians or philosophers."

159:4.6 "The thing most deplorable is not merely this erroneous idea of the absolute perfection of the Scripture record and the infallibility

70

of its teachings, but rather the confusing misinterpretation of these sacred writings by the tradition-enslaved scribes and Pharisees at Jerusalem. And now will they employ both the doctrine of the inspiration of the Scriptures and their misinterpretations thereof in their determined effort to withstand these newer teachings of the gospel of the kingdom. Nathaniel, never forget, the Father does not limit the revelation of truth to any one generation or to any one people. Many earnest seekers after the truth have been, and will continue to be, confused and disheartened by these doctrines of the perfection of the Scriptures."

159:4.7 "The authority of truth is the very spirit that indwells its living manifestations, and not the dead words of the less illuminated and supposedly inspired men of another generation. And even if these holy men of old lived inspired and spirit-filled lives, that does not mean that their words were similarly spiritually inspired. Today we make no record of the teachings of this gospel of the kingdom lest, when I have gone, you speedily become divided up into sundry groups of truth contenders as a result of the diversity of your interpretation of my teachings. For this generation it is best that we live these truths while we shun the making of records."

159:4.8 "Mark you well my words, Nathaniel, nothing which human nature has touched can be regarded as infallible. Through the mind of man divine truth may indeed shine forth, but always of relative purity and partial divinity. The creature may crave infallibility, but only the Creators possess it."

159:4.9 "But the greatest error of the teaching about the Scriptures is the doctrine of their being sealed books of mystery and wisdom which only the wise minds of the nation dare to interpret. The revelations of divine truth are not sealed except by human ignorance, bigotry, and narrow-minded intolerance. The light of the Scriptures is only dimmed by prejudice and darkened by superstition. A false fear of sacredness has prevented religion from being safeguarded by common sense. The fear of the authority of the sacred writings of the past effectively prevents the honest souls of today from accepting the new light of the gospel, the light which these very God-knowing men of another generation so intensely longed to see."

159:4.10 "But the saddest feature of all is the fact that some of the teachers of the sanctity of this traditionalism know this very truth. They more or less fully understand these limitations of Scripture, but they are moral cowards, intellectually dishonest. They know the truth regarding the sacred writings, but they prefer to withhold such disturbing facts from the people. And thus do they pervert and distort the Scriptures, making them the guide to slavish details of the daily life and an authority in things nonspiritual instead of appealing to the sacred writings as the repository of the moral wisdom, religious inspiration, and the spiritual teaching of the God-knowing men of other generations."

159:4.11 Nathaniel was enlightened, and shocked, by the Master's pronouncement. He long pondered this talk in the depths of his soul, but he told no man concerning this conference until after Jesus' ascension; and even then he feared to impart the full story of the Master's instruction.

Love Energy of the Heart

Many people are not prepared to give up what they have considered to be truth. They are always looking for ways to confirm and to define and to show what they believe is correct, so there is an insatiable desire by many souls to know the futility of arguing over scripture. There is no absolute correctness of any kind on the earth plane or elsewhere because truth is relative. It is the energy itself, existing and flowing, part of the beingness that all souls know as God – that is what people are truly after: their own experience of the love connection. Anyone who tells you otherwise is, of course, lost in their own need to define and their own need to know. Accept the difference in viewpoints. The greater mission here is in utilizing the heart energy to take you to a far more astute place.

Many spiritual people of this generation are attempting to bridge the fields of religion, science, and psychology to find a common ground and work together to find a more peaceful way of living on this earth. The Institute of HeartMath Research Center is a group exploring how we are all globally interconnected at a deep, fundamental level via electromagnetic fields and biofields. Did you know that your heart, not your brain, is the organ of your body that produces the most energy? As measured by an EKG, the electrical current of the heart is 60 times stronger than that of the brain. The electromagnetic field of your heart can be detected up to 15 feet away from the body. Talk about a big communicating Aura.

Your heart is much more than a pump that provides blood circulation. Your heart has many complex functions. The heart is an endocrine gland that produces hormones. It houses a sophisticated nervous system, the "little brain of the heart," that gathers information, communicates, and has its own intelligence. The intelligence of your brain is different from that of your heart and plays a different role. Recent research in the field of neuro-cardiology has improved our understanding of the respective roles of the brain and the heart. Scientists have long recognized that the brain has the power to influence the heart. Researchers have now proved that the heart has the power to modulate brain activity and to optimize its function.

Scientists describe a state of well-being, called cardiac coherence, obtained by synchronizing the brain and the heart, which yields remarkable benefits in the areas of health, personal energy, and relationships. Connecting to this love energy in meditation is easy. You can try a bio-feedback device or brain / heart-sync CD.

Chemicals of Emotions

Therefore, while it is true that the emotional brain, known as the Limbic System, is a grouping of related components surrounding the brain-stem and laying beneath the neocortex, it can also be thought of as a whole body system, too. The Hypothalamus, Amygdala, and Hippocampus have distinct activities and properties which work collectively in the human brain to provide emotion, motivation, and memory association.

Candace Pert, author of *The Molecules of Emotions: Life Science Behind the Mind Body Connection* was a pharmacologist and lead investigator into ways that the mind talks with the body. Her research on how the chemicals inside our bodies form a dynamic information network, linking mind and body, was ground breaking. Emotions are neuropeptides attaching to receptors and stimulating an electrical change on neurons. The mind exists not only in the brain, but outside as well Neuropeptides are also produced by the spleen, thymus, bone marrow, lymph glands, and the dorsal horn of the spine. Neuropeptides produced by the brain, arriving to open receptors in the intestines, are the root of the expression 'gut feeling.' There is a bio-chemical link between the mind and body within this communicative network.

In theory, no emotion is wrong to have. However, anyone in the midst of a crying jig knows that it doesn't feel that great. Stopping the tears feels good and so does the release of pent up energy. Research shows that the emotional chemicals that are released can be habit forming and that a person can become almost addicted to these chemicals. The movie, *What the Bleep Do We Know?*, has a scene about this action which is quite humorous. At a wedding, the guys wanting dates found girls, the angry lady found something to be upset about, and the betrayed photographer assumed the groom was already cheating.

Homeostasis is the process of returning your emotions to normal because your body wants to feel good. Sweeping situations that cause distress under the rug will not change repeating patterns. After your emotions are on an even keel, begin to examine the source of conflict. Check for Memes and expectations.

Watch How We Label

Observing and shifting unhelpful thoughts is using our knowledge of what is called "The Law of Attraction." We wish to use our thoughts and emotions to attract positive experiences. Simple reframing you can do on your own goes like this, "I always mess-up when it is important...wait a second...that is not true ...let me think of something positive to say to myself...OK I may have gotten a later start then I wanted this morning but at least I am in the car now...let me think of the best route to get there...boy I am catching all the green lights...I wonder when I first heard or felt that I mess-up when it is important...that sure was a powerful emotion I felt when I said that to myself...I sure did a good job shifting my thoughts and emotions...look at that: I see a good parking spot right up front."

Watching how we label thoughts, emotions, and experiences is the key to allowing the love energy flow through our lives without restrictions. Often what happens in an energy exchange is beyond words and has many facets. The caution surrounding labeling could apply to all we choose to name, like diseases and even healing modalities. For example, when a client feels energy or heat coming from my hands they may ask what I am doing. I may choose to call it Reiki energy because I have learned, been attuned, and granted the proficiency title of Master. However, labeling it as Reiki, could limit what I allow others to know what I bring to them because such an emanation of vibration as the word Reiki limits what I am doing in the mind of the client.

When people come off my table they are changed, whether from the massage or hypnosis session. They have put their earthly issues on the hanger like their clothes. Our energies have merged and an energy exchange has taken place. How long the peaceful state will last truly depends on how long they can avoid attaching themselves to outside thought forms and responsibilities. Often, I jokingly grant them permission to do nothing the rest of the day. At our soulful core, we are peace and calm. We do have the choice to which memes and beliefs we want to preserve. All the things on our to-do list seem trivial in comparison to the feeling of the love energy thread connection. Our thinking and the words we communicate with have an effect on our emotions. Sometimes thinking is just over rated. ☺

Emotional Opportunities

The advice to watch how we label is amplified as we discuss our emotions. They are so personal and are felt in the moment. The scale of emotions range from Love to Fear and have many nuances in between. Emotional hijacking occurs when a person's mind gets taken over by his or her emotions and inhibits him or her from viewing a situation realistically. It may lead to a cognitive loss of control and can be harmful or even murderous. The Teachings of Abraham channeled by Esther Hicks suggests that we reach for a thought that brings us **up** "The Emotional Guidance Scale" to improve our vibrations, in her book, *Ask and It is Given*.

Love	Peace	Passion	Happiness
Hopefulness	Contentment/ Calm	Acceptance	Boredom
Frustration/ Jealousy	Hopeless/ Worry	Anger/ Revenge	Fear

David Hawkins, author of *Power vs. Force,* has determined through kinesiology research that a person's emotions may come and go but the average person's level of consciousness remains rather steady throughout his or her lifetime. The level is governed by specific energy fields in the

79

nonlinear domain. However, if one desires to raise consciousness, it is possible to have the level of calibrated consciousness jump hundreds of points in a lifetime.

Is there constant judgment in your mind? Our physicality and our divinity are so tied up and interwoven into our being that we really are recognizing our divinity in difficult moments. We are capable of experiencing the full range of emotions. Most would say they want to bring forth the highest and best way of feeling. However, there is equal value in recognizing the collective nature of life when feeling the emotions of anger, jealousy, or envy. All emotions bring about an instantaneous opportunity to move into the more loving way of being. Therefore, in turn, they become gifts as well. *Do you feel justified in expressing your frustration onto others? Or do you accept and take responsibility for what it is you are feeling? Often, I find it is a meme or hidden expectation that elicits the reactive response from my ego. Journal about your last meltdown.*

Dark Night of the Soul

How is it that we can be feeling our wondrous nature in one second and in the next feel the darkness and the depths of being in the pits of humanity? The term dark night of the soul is when you feel lost, ungrounded, and abandoned. Many people assume, and often mistake, this feeling for depression, or that it emerges into one's life following an emotional crisis, such as divorce. But a dark night will often enter a person's life in the midst of their most joyous time after achieving an anticipated goal. In time, living with your creation may feel flat, so what's next?

A few things could be going on here. Overwhelming feelings about responsibilities can begin to foster the idea that if there has to be one more activity or one more investment in something to even think about, let alone do, that there will just be an implosion, a breakup of the whole psyche. When there is too much choice and data to be analyzed, stillness is required to determine what is important. Paring down on activities to create some space in your schedule allows time to reflect.

We are connected to the collective nature of the whole human experience and so sometimes we are feeling the emotions of others, especially those of us who are greatly empathic. The movement of emotion could be tapping into a realm of experience, which does not fit into a level that is known. There are always more impacts, more energetic exchanges, more influences coming from so many different dimensions than we can possibly realize.

Carolyn Myss' audio lecture, *Spiritual Madness*, asks the audience to question if they feel their spiritual efforts should be rewarded and how much is just personal ambition. When the voice of guidance suddenly stops, do you experience the breakdown of your concepts of the Divine? Are you expecting God to solve problems that you need to do for yourself? She feels the journey is not about controlling what you get but embracing whatever comes. The job is to master your responses to external events, not attempt to control them.

Like the seasons, this winter-like energy will change. "With this signal, I wonder what this means about where I am going now and how the ceiling I have lived under for so long is being raised." This period is about submitting yourself to the love energy flow and realizing you are going to have situations and episodes in your physical life that will feel flat. Be patient with yourself and practice nurturing self-care. After a season, making a decision will usher in a new wave of excitement.

The Soul's Perspective on the Ego and Mind

Who is running the show? There is a braiding of experience going on here. There is nothing manmade that ties the ego to the soul. The ego and the soul are, of course, completely intertwined and overlapped together, so it is not a matter of judging who is doing what. Embrace the wondrous nature of the totality of your beingness with no need to put them into separate compartments. You can't separate that which is so inclusive and divine and yet we have the illusion that we can.

From a soul's perspective what does matter here is that the love energy is funneled through a system that is working in top notch order. Whatever you can do to contribute to that, whatever you can create that would allow the physicality to be at its highest functioning level, is all that is required. Each soul, in its own proclivity of physicality, must attend to whatever is occurring within that sensitive bodily functioning. That includes the mind as well. If there is a mind that's capability is stronger, higher, or more aware, the illusions of achievement could result in a perceived separateness but really the mind has agreed and becomes a part of the experience and is not in any way trying to be a barrier to oneness.

This really is why so many feel stuck. They cannot take themselves front and center, confronting their minds and allowing their energy to go beyond what the mind has insisted it is for and what it functions as. This is why there is so much intrusion or disease in other areas of the physical nature - the mind is kept set in a particular way here. With all that is required to fit in socially, the mind becomes stationary and so set to be culturally acceptable. How can the body make its own leap into what is the highest level of functioning if the mind is thus keeping it at a lower level?

The trance state can bring out what the mind has hidden to a more conscious fashion, to put some sort of order and focus which, in turn, then helps in the communicative process of the physical being. However, there is nothing that inhibits the functioning of co-operation at the level of love energy between body and soul. There is such a dense language and thick covering of beliefs and thinking which cause the illusion. This is why I felt such an expansion and melding of experience going on inside myself as I wrote about this material over the past ten years because there is a dichotomy going on from what the soul feels is important and what I had been taught as a child and learned at the university. *How have you consciously blended the wisdom from within and allowed it to be expressed?*

84

Decision Making

From the soul's perspective, *there is no choice.* Choice is in the mind of the human being. You feel better, you feel freer, and you feel as if there is some measure of control when you can accept choice but that, of course, is not so. Choice has everything to do with how the human mind functions and very little to do with what the experience of the love energy is.

When you are tussling between what is most astute for you spiritually and what you feel is best for you physically – you know immediately that something is off. For example, you must decide what to do. Shall you take a walk or meditate? It is not as astute as it can be if you feel it has to be one or the other. What you recognize is that both are required, both are important, and both bring you to a level of awareness that's the ultimate joining, the ultimate recognition of love, and the divinity of being.

So you have to ask yourself, "Which is it, in the moment, that I will give over to? Which in the moment, then, will I do in a different moment?" That's exactly what is called for here - not which one, one or the other, excluding one to go with the other – to recognize both are balanced into the entire experience of who you are. In that moment, it would be safe to say that it matters not which one you go to in that moment, laying down to the astral plane or getting up and walking with the wind at your face, and giving you that recognition you are, indeed, a part of the whole of Gaia. Both are important. Both are necessary, and you must accommodate both. How you do it, when you do it, and with what fervor you do it becomes your choice. It's one of the adventures of being in the human consciousness. Simply don't see it as one or the other. It's both and how you carry it out is your decision. The connection is the same and so there is no choice.

If guilt steps in, then you know clearly somewhere within your will you've made up your mind not to do the other. If you are in no way going to dismiss the other activity, then you simply recognize the next moment will bring that opportunity, so where is there room for guilty? Guilt only builds on your decision with the will to not do something so when you realize that guilt is there, you must ask yourself, "Why has that crept in? What have I decided in my willful way that this needs to come forward as a choice?" In that moment, then, be rid of it because you will immediately say, "It is not that I'm not going to go walk. I am going to go walk. It's just that not this moment. So be gone guilt, be still mind, and go another route."

Willfulness

Willfulness is such a part of this experience in human form. There is nothing that can dispel the will, by any means, nor would you want to. The will allows you to feel and to experience that which is happening in the physical and integrate it into the *loving soul energy.* The challenge is to take your willfulness, recognize it has a purpose, examine what it is that you are doing with it, and let go of your need to see it come out a different way, a particular way, or a certain and written in stone way. When you can release your need to have it manifest in a particular way, then your willfulness takes on a more soulful approach. It begins to go with whatever the flow is, the fluidity of experience makes itself manifest. That, in itself, requires the complicity of the will.

So do not feel as if the will must be dismantled or somehow dismissed. Allow the will to come in but not in the way that you expect or hold on to outcomes. Simply allow the will to be a vehicle to take you to the level of the soul knowing that this is what you want and this is what you need and what all souls are asking for. Then you will lose your need to have it come in a particular way and will begin to see it as something that allows you to experience life in a more feeling manner.

I'm reminded of Garth Brook's song, "Unanswered Prayers," where the lyrics say that some of God's greatest gifts are unanswered prayers. We don't know what is around the corner, and that is why it is wise to intend for what we want or something better for all those involved. There is a different ring to I WILL then to I AM. I am intending to accomplish this task. It gives you the option to be in the moment and experience what the moment brings without controlling the outcome. Many wonderful moments happen spontaneously and may have a better feel then the long prepared event.

We have to be reminded that it is not the thinking of the mind that brings us to what we truly want. What we desire is the feeling of love and peace. The excitement we feel does get triggered by the mind but frustration can also be at play when circumstances don't go our way. The experience and journey is where the love energy lies, not in the outcome, not in the effects, not in the results. There is much fear and anxiety surrounding the ability to measure up to one's peers. The Dali Lama says, "The planet does not need more 'successful people.' The planet desperately needs more peacemakers, healers, restorers, storytellers, and lovers of all kinds."

Peace of Fearing Not

The words of Dr. Joe Vitale made an impression on me when I sat in the audience during the National Guild of Hypnotist convention. He said he would teach us how we can never have to worry about making money again. I remember little else of the presentation but at the end he repeated, "You never have to worry about money or anything else again. Ever. Well, you don't. But you can if you want to." Change is going to happen; however, fearing the process is optional. Here is a list of common fears. Is yours on here? Living in South Florida, we get used to lizards and large palmetto bugs. Where do these fears originate?

Failure	Death	Rejection	Doctors
Public Speaking	Ridicule	Snakes	Heights
Pain	Flying in a plane	Dogs	Small spaces
Roller coasters	Swimming	Spiders	Being Trapped
Being late	Loss of freedom	Mice	The unknown

Most worries of the mind do not come into physical reality. Repetitive thoughts can be paralyzing. So how do we deal with this stuck energy? Feel it, don't shift it at first. *Ask yourself what is truly going on here. Write out the problem and brainstorm ideas, crazy as they may seem. This process gives you hope that there are options.* So you have to sleep with the raccoons for a night outside. Having lived through it, the next time that you see a move coming you will have the knowledge that you are stronger that you think you are. You may learn to ask for help or connect sooner to other options. Shows like *Naked and Afraid* give us appreciation for our Paleolithic past.

"There are two basic motivating forces: fear and love. When we are afraid, we pull back from life. When we are in love, we open to all that life has to offer with passion, excitement, and acceptance. We need to learn to love ourselves first, in all our glory and our imperfections. If we cannot love ourselves, we cannot fully open to our ability to love others or our potential to create. Evolution and all hopes for a better world rest in the fearlessness and open-hearted vision of people who embrace life." — John Lennon

Chapter 4:

What now?

I am love

I am light

I am still

I am ready

Watch me now

How much excitement do you need to feel alive? Our soul comes into physicality to experience humanity. Why are you still here? What draws you to the earth plane? This chapter discusses the energy of intentions and goals. What do you feel adds to and gives enrichment to your life? Learn how to manifest your heart's desire and feel the love energy thread from all realms in the process.

The objective is to awaken the knowing and intuitive aspect of yourself by having you feel the loving connection of self, communities, and dimensions. Grow your confidence as you move from apprentice to master. You will find many opportunities to use this information within yourself. You are here to awaken the power in the moment and manifest a strong conscious connection to ALL THAT IS. Allow yourself to feel the immenseness of that, the grandness of that journey, and give yourself credit for what it is you are accomplishing.

Live from a place of what feels astute to you. You do not *need* to do anything but experience the pleasure of physicality. Claim the parts of your experience which gives a sense of knowing that love is truly the "soul" reason for incarnating.

Stillness

Why is it when I am at work, I long to be off work, at home, or on a trip? And when I am at the beach and I am looking at the beautiful ocean, why do I wonder what worthwhile task should I do when I leave? And yet, I know intellectually it matters not where I am when I breathe and feel peace and a surge of the love energy within. The mind wants to give a story to this stillness. For a moment there is silence, gratitude, and excitement all together at the center. Any random thoughts are like clouds shifting and changing, just being observed.

There are some that hold the benchmark of stillness and nirvana as a place to strive for. Yes, there are benefits to finding the blissful state. However the striving for something is counter effective, for lack of can bring forth frustration, jealousy, and a sense of less than. We all return to this place when we sleep anyway. Formal practices to induce the stillness of trance can be gotten from meditation, yoga, prayer, shamanic journeys, and belly breathing.

Everyday monotonous activities can also relax the mind and give us this state of stillness and bliss. The late Annie Luther had such an experience of bliss while peeling potatoes at the kitchen sink. Recognizing and acknowledging these moments will tend to increase their frequency. There is no need to live in a monastery to find this place. It is there for us all to enjoy and use. It is like the European Piazzas where you never know who or what will show up.

There are some of us that go through longer periods of time in this state. Eckhart Tolle, the author of *The Power of Now,* had a profound awaking after his 29th birthday when he was in the pits of emotional trauma. His transformation and his awareness left him blissfully sitting on park benches enjoying nature because no activity could give him anything more than what he was experiencing. As this feeling became normalized after five months, he began to respond to peoples' request for guidance and quite naturally became a spiritual teacher.

What takes you out of this state of bliss can be just as simple as the body's call back, "I'm hungry or I need to use the bathroom." Moments of stillness can give us inspiration and random ideas, some exciting that we can take action on.

Exciting Goals and Projects

So what is the next step or activity after one has awareness about self and his or her place in the oneness of life? Perhaps it is not the goal itself that is most important but the quality of the energy and effort going forth which matters most. Do you feel you have carte blanche to do as you feel fit, as long as you do it with love, connection, humor and excitement? *"Aude Aliquid Dignum"* is to "Dare Something Worthy." The spirit of the Bodhisattva Vow is to be of service to all sentient beings until nirvana is experienced by all, not just in this lifetime, but in all future ones as well. Somewhere in that mix is an exciting idea to be birthed.

Setting intentions and writing down goals allows the energy to build and keeps the mind focused. Goals can be broken into do-able steps that are accomplishable. Ask yourself what has to happen for you to achieve the goal. Believe that if you continue to build momentum and act on the tasks at hand, you will succeed. The use of positive affirmations that are short, simply stated for immediate action will remind you what needs to be done to benefit your short or long term goals. For example: "Every day before I leave the house in the morning I write three pages and feel excited that the first draft of my book is finished in three months." "Every day I prepare healthy food to take with me

95

so that my body is nourished and I feel fit." Notice how these thoughts are positive, present tense, and measurable?

Choose thoughts that align with your goals because they are followed by feelings and chemicals that affect behaviors. Awareness of self-talk and the ability to shift negative thinking to a believable positive alternative is the process of finishers. When you can close your eyes and imagine yourself accomplishing your goals and taking the small action steps required, you are pre-paving the way. The suggestions are reinforcement by visualizing the behaviors and are believable. We can use the internal and external motivators to our advantage. The most helpful attractor is focusing on how the process feels. Feel the love and excitement.

Practice writing a "Statements of Intent" in your journal now. K.I.S.S.: Keep It Simple Smarty; then let your imagination fly with ideas, both silly and practical. Feel the energy surrounding your idea and take one action towards it.

Getting Started

Don't let the search for a worthy action immobilize you with no action for fear of doing the wrong thing. Know that the next moment will lead to another opportunity for action. Most of the time, it is the feeling of being overwhelmed that prevents the first step of action. Does your task or goal seem too big? Break it down into smaller activities. Is there a childish voice inside that says, "I don't feel like it?" Then you may have to use the distraction method to get started.

This may mean to just start moving, opening your eyes, stretching, getting out of bed, taking a shower, and just getting dressed. Read your to-do list and allow yourself to do something simple, make coffee or tea, then clean your purse or nightstand. Don't judge your movements, the order, or if you get distracted by another activity, as long as you put it on the list. Let the vortex of action continue. I call this method of getting things done the "bounce method." By moving around the house randomly, but with purpose, feels free and creative. Harder or more difficult items on the list seem easier when I am in motion and my Virgo tendencies towards completion have silenced any discussion of, "If I feel like it."

I'm also a big fan of the "Have Done List" because when you are in bounce mode, you end up doing a lot more than your original to-do list. Al Secunda, author of *The 15-Second Principle,* has lots of suggestions for actualizing our dreams. He acknowledges there are preparatory steps to items on the to-do list. You may need to write that e-mail; however, the reason that you may not have started it yet is because you need to find the business card that has the address on it first. Is it mixed in the pile of papers on the desk, in your purse, or in the console of your car? Finding the business card is really another step to finishing the task.

Don't underestimate the power of the momentum. When I was 22 years old, I was inspired by a store that I visited while on vacation. I was curious to see what it would cost to replicate such a store in my area, so I checked out retail space, looked into suppliers, and applied for credit. Then I was doing it: signing a lease, designing the floor plan, and creating a logo. As my friend Mike says, "If you don't want a haircut don't hang around a barbershop." ***Take one goal step today.***

Self-Sabotage

So what is really going on when you start and stop your projects? Was there more time and effort required than what you had planned? Did you get distracted or did the small boring monotonous details wane your desire? Did something more important come along or did you do all you could do and now are waiting on other circumstances that are not under your control? The quicker that you correctly assess the situation with honest feedback, the better you feel and take the most helpful action.

We use the words "Self-Sabotage" when we feel we covertly stop our progress. The hidden fear of success can cause us to secretly want to keep things the same. If everything you consider worthwhile is hinging on this "project" then what happens when you're done? What if nothing changes or everything and everyone I now love changes? This fear of the unknown or "mini death" can stymie and paralyze action towards completion. Avoiding completion then has a purpose, it is a mind trick. Figure out the hidden fears and move forward with love.

Postponing the joy and love that is available to you now does not make sense, but that is what we secretly do. Fall in love with the process of achieving your goals and marvel at the synchronicity and beauty along the way. Notice the support that is around you. It may be that short conversation with a stranger that gives you the resolve to continue. You may need to feel uncomfortable in your stretch, as you juggle many hats, and transmute that diluted feeling to one of satisfaction.

Guard your time and learn to say, "Not now, I'll get back to you when I can." Steven Covey's quote, "You have to decide what your highest priorities are and have the courage – pleasantly, smilingly, non-apologetically - to say 'no' to other things. And the way you do that is by having a bigger 'yes' burning inside. The enemy of the best is often the good," is in a Plexiglas holder on my desk. Reducing the amount of relaxation time watching entertainment just makes sense. Do you really want to watch a bunch of strangers compete and complete tasks for prizes or do you want to accomplish your own dreams and be the leading lady or leading man in your own life? Are you constantly allowing yourself to be bombarded by programming and corporate ads that do not reflect your values and distract you from taking meaningful action? *Choose to spend your time and money in the same direction as your values and goals. Journal now about your intentions and see if you feel excitement or if there is any resistance or negative thinking.*

Getting the Support of the Mind

The unconscious mind holds the key to the part of us that is sabotaging our goals. There may just be a part of us that is fearful, negative, and is controlling the process of finishing. Imagine that you are at a board meeting and all your aspects are present: Ms. Together, Bossy Bertha, Toni the Tour Guide, Accounting Annie, Negative Nancy, Cheerleader Cheri, Helpful Hannah, Fearful Granny, Confident Connie, etc. Allow them to brainstorm together to come up with creative ideas to move forward with ease. Ms. Together and Confident Connie may need to assure Fearful Granny and Accounting Annie with a plan and budget that makes sense to get their co-operation. Sometimes the opinions we hear are from other people, and they can be transmuted by examining, confronting, and declaring our resolve. Author David Quiggley, *Alchemical Hypnotherapy,* calls this process the "Conference Room" and has seen there are no limits to what a person can achieve when aspects of the psyche are united behind a single purpose and external controlling influences are eliminated.

The act of visualizing your desired outcomes helps to program the mind to attract what you already have seen yourself experiencing. Pre-paving your day is a ritual that I have my clients practice. The best time to start this is ideally when you are still in bed, still in the dreamy state. Allow yourself to pretend and imagine:

1. Pick out what you are going to wear. See yourself getting dressed.
2. Imagine getting all your waking tasks done easy.
3. Remember all the items you need to bring with you before you leave the house for the day.
4. Imagine having fun and feeling joyous as you complete all your tasks for the day, easily and effortlessly. The day goes smoothly and you feel lucky.
5. Feel the energy move through your body as you take three deep breaths and open your eyes feeling refreshed and excited about the start of your new day. Enjoy the synchronicities

End of day ritual: Feel gratitude as you re-experience, review, and re-frame your day before you drift off to sleep. Make peace and release. You are blessed and loved. Any concerns are worked out while you rest. All is well; you are safe.

Facing the Unexpected

The unexpected can come at once like the death of a close family member, friend, or pet. Some changes are out of our control because of changing trends or market conditions. My shift into the healing profession came about after I got my MBA degree in August of 2001, the next month saw a change in the markets with the uncertainty of the events from 9/11. That morning, my telephone interview for a human resources job in Washington, D.C. was cancelled. I continued to substitute teach and work for the Boys and Girls Club until I enrolled in massage school the following year. And then I learned hypnosis the year after that.

Having the attitude and confidence that you can handle what the moment brings is most important when the unexpected happens. When visiting my Nana on the other coast of Florida in June of 2009, I got a phone call that woke me from a dead sleep. The property manager was calling to say that there was a fire at my day spa business. The fire sprinklers went off and soaked everything. It was 6:00 a.m., and I had planned to sleep in because I was up until 3:00 a.m. reading the new book I had bought, *Does This Clutter Make my Butt Look Fat,* by Peter Walsh. Just a few hours before I was envisioning how I wanted my life to be, ironic right?

When I got back into town, I was determined to keep a positive attitude and not go down that path of "poor me." Being displaced while the repairs were made gave me a breath of fresh energy and got me moving around the community to find a temporary location to work out of. If there was lemonade to be made out of this sour situation, I was bound and determined to do so. That summer did bring me opportunities to connect with new people, take a few classes, and I found a new location to relocate to that was much lower in rent.

Business stability was mine for about 20 months until my city took some of that Stimulus Money and closed the road in front of my shop in downtown Boca Raton for three months to put new electric, plumbing, and pavers down to give the area a facelift. Not wanting to subject clients to the dust and drilling, we were closed during the day. I had therapists for evening and weekend appointments, and I took off to California for a temporary consulting and mystery shopping assignment. Yes, another glass of lemonade.

What's So Funny?

Opportunity for new experiences is what the unexpected brings to us. The saying the "best laid plans of mice and men often go wrong" got its origin from the feeling poet Robert Burns had when he upturned a mouse nest while plowing a field. The plans we make promising joy may end up bringing grief and pain. It is in our seeing the humor in the situation that can restore the joy that was the desired result in the first place.

As you face the world of the human being, there has been a long standing recognition by those who have stepped into the lightness of life that laughter is an essential ingredient. Humor, itself, is the very heart of being on this earth and surviving with all aspects intact. Those of you that have walked this plane and have been a part of it in so many different ways, from so many different angles, know this. So you will each find your own way to lighten, to laugh, to find the humor in existence and then play it for all it's worth. That is what souls, such as Robin Williams and Joan Rivers, turned themselves over to completely.

Comedy clubs and funny movies provide a place and opportunity that's whole purpose is to make another laugh. Laughter is an essential ingredient to finding the joy in being in human form. Just as your vehicles need to pull up to the gasoline pump, souls can pull up to the energy of laughter and feel sustained. While I was in California on assignment, I got the opportunity to experience the comedy business by befriending a few comedians and assisting in several promotional events. This emerging and exciting career twist bought me back to California to live for a year. My foray into that world was short but being able to taste and participate behind the scenes was sufficient at that time.

Have you ever noticed that you can express even difficult conversations with another if you can keep it light? Many public speakers use self-deprecating humor to build rapport with their audiences on purpose. Humor can relieve tension and pave the way to better communication. Getting the flow going starts first with ourselves and not taking everything so seriously. With a little reframing work, we can find most clouds have a funny silver lining.

Asking for Help

Keeping your sense of humor is most helpful when your efforts to be self-reliant are thwarted or the unexpected catches you in need. There are times when we must ask for help. If you have been the type of person who has been more of a giver than a taker, then this change of energy may feel uncomfortable. View this hardship as an opportunity to connect to the greater love that is there for you. Correctly assess the dilemma and determine how much help you need in time, money, or favors.

The practice of getting yourself into that trance-like state can bring big dividends here. Use your imagination to see many possible outcomes to your situation. Pre-pave conversations asking for help. Notice what or who comes to mind in these sessions. Let people know of your need and ask them if they have any ideas. They may know someone who can help or point you in the right direction. There may even be help found in community organizations.

Most situations are just temporary and provide opportunities for learning and growth. Your healthy pride can stay intact as you graciously accept the help and allow the astute love energy thread to come full circle. When you do nice things for others, sometimes they are in the position to reciprocate at another time, but it is not always the person that you help who ends up stepping up to the plate. Allow and claim the help that the universe provides for you. Saying thank-you and feeling grateful keeps the flow of energy going. Your frame of mind is the attraction point so keep it positive.

How much of a savings account do you need when you trust in the universe? Mildred Norman was a woman who walked more than 25,000 miles from 1953 to 1981 and called herself the "Peace Pilgrim." She trusted in the love connection of the universe and ate and slept when food and lodging was offered to her. She dared something worthy and knew her value was greater than any amount in a savings account could be. Think of all the people she touched with her message of hope and peace. She was able to gracefully accept help and handle fluctuations in her resources. When we turn ourselves over to the depths of our soul, there will bound to be periods the external world hopes to catch up.

What Feels Astute?

You do not *need* anything so don't go after something from a place of need. Do it from a place of what feels astute to you. What do you feel adds and gives enrichment to your life? Whatever those aspects are in the physical, by all means take them with you. Claim them as parts of your experience that which gives you not only pleasure but a sense of knowing what this incarnational life is about. Whatever that is take hold of it, let it be a part of you. If it calls to not be with you any longer then let it go.

It's not as if everything is constant. Are there certain things now in this moment that you would claim as important and enriching to you in the way of physicality that you wouldn't have five years ago? Of course! There are aspects now of what you consider to be important and essential for you physically that you didn't even know existed five years ago and there will be more going forward. It just simply moves that way. It only becomes an encumbrance and something that you become upset, angry, or hurt about when you feel that you have to have it, when you sense that your happiness is dependent upon it. Know that when you begin to look at every move you make without need and without dependency, without requirement, then you can find with pleasure to take what you want as a physical being.

109

Being able to release what you no longer use frees up the space around you. The accumulation of excessive material goods has given birth to the Self-Storage industry. Fears of being without have made some hoard and live in homes that are health hazards. Releasing is challenging when downsizing and moving into smaller quarters. Less is better when you have faith and the wisdom to acknowledge new manifestations and experiences are on the horizon. Energy abhors a vacuum so make space for the new.

De-cluttering is helpful with your schedule, too. Was the taste of an activity enough for you? As a kid, my dad took us to watch him fly a plane. I always wondered why he stopped taking lessons. I took some lessons myself in the late 1990s and after 6½ hours logged, I counted the cost and decided to use my money instead to buy a house. Some activities are just meant to be temporary and some goals are to be adjusted, postponed, or eliminated to reflect your current desires and circumstances. An effective way to attract something you do want is to make room for the new and harmonize your attitude.

The New Human

Life cycles effect people, businesses, and civilizations. We grow from infant, child, young adult, mature, to elderly in our human life cycle. Businesses and civilizations have a similar cycle: start up, growth, maturity, and decline. Now the decline can bring death or a rebirth of activity which continues the cycle with new growth. The human DNA and our civilization are in this rebirth period. We have collectively decided to stay. The truth of this shift is real; Many are willing to look at life, perhaps, from a different perspective than they have allowed before.

After leaving an attraction at an Orlando theme park in the fall of 2009, I got this overwhelming feeling of disinterest in the repetitive storyline of good vs. evil. All the rides seemed the same, the same story. It was like the never changing result of a tic tac toe game. The "Hero's Journey" is the same predetermined path which the movie and book industry use to move a story along. Variety and new plots, after the brass ring is gotten, are needed. How does the hero / master live after enlightenment in today's world? What is Cinderella's life like, happily ever after? What happens after nirvana? After we heal, can we see the change reflected back to us in the faces of those we mistook for adversaries?

The intellect which has dominated our actions is receding as the love of the heart is emerging as we connect with compassion. Our long held beliefs are being examined for their value. Releasing outdated memes which bind gives a sense of freedom and lightness. We do know our thoughts affect our outer reality, but human limits are not clearly known. As one runner beats the world's record for time, another runner soon matches and surpasses it. How this growth in human consciousness shows itself in your own life is individualistic. It may be the increase in synchronicities, being woken up before your alarm goes off, looking at the clock and seeing your favorite number, or routinely getting a good parking spot.

The souls that incarnate now are already equipped with a stronger sixth sense and ability for multi-dimensional communications. They are a group that loves collaboration and have embraced connecting technology. A new human chapter has begun. We don't have to fall into the same emotional dramas. We can pick our responses, allowing a moment to vent or grieve if that is what is needed, but our innocence has past. We will never fit in the little chair at the kids' table any longer. We can shore up to the wondrous expansion of consciousness as we put away childish beliefs and fears, ready to embrace our powerful loving connection.

Building a Soulful Community

You are now experiencing your upgrade in expanded consciousness. Allow enough down time in your weekly schedule to be able to put your to do list away and fall into the energy of the moment. Listen to the energy itself as it calls to you and in that moment fall into it. This sensation is important because you realize that it is fall into - it's not suddenly harness, take the reins up, direct, orchestrate, move in a particular direction, get your map, get your plan, and go with security and safety. You can be a pioneer willing to say, "The wagons must go – no more reins." The illusion of control is what we have lived under as humans for eons. Society has socialized us into a common way of being that is not absolute and so in the moment of unstructured time, there are hidden surprises.

One of the benefits after the post 9/11 slowdown in the economy was the schedule that substitute teaching afforded me. I was home to watch *Oprah* and learn from her amazing guests. Gary Zukav, Debbie Ford, and Cheryl Richardson are three that I still remember watching. Cheryl's book, *Take Time for Your Life,* influenced my educational path by the Coach U reference in her book. The concept of building a soulful community on purpose has stayed with me, too.

"Building a soulful community of friends is an important and strategic part of living a life that honors your authentic self."

Finding a group of people to support and reflect back to you your true self is a worthwhile pursuit. You may fall into such connections as you go about your daily routine. Random conversations may turn into something more. Be open to making new friends. Inviting new people into your life is not about the quantity but about the quality of heart connection. Mr. Rogers" opening song invites us to be his neighbor. His program was a good example of how to interact in a healthy, happy way in our communities. Who is in your soulful community?

As we finish this volume about self, we weave the love energy thread into the fabric which includes others. We will open the discussion on the relationships we have with others and how to lovingly interact within our communities in volume two. The third volume will be about the connection between us and the energies that are not human. All have the opportunity to reflex back to us *LOVE*.

Appendix: Pendulum and Soul Charts

Using a Pendulum

Your skill at getting in a trance state is going to help you in learning how to use a pendulum for getting information from your subconscious mind / higher-self and your super conscious mind / other worldly energies. The ego takes a back seat here and moves over so that communication comes through from outside your conscious awareness.

Setting the Environment/Ritual

- Be Comfortable
- Quiet Area
- Candles & Incense
- Clear mind, ask for guides, say prayer or mantra
- Ask guides to "gate keep"

Getting Started

- Yes / No movement
- Simple Charts
- Soul Charts
- Letter Board
- Jumping off: hearing, feeling, seeing

- Recording
- Channeling for others

Be patient with yourself while you are learning this process. Everyone has the ability to experience connecting in this way. The connection gets stronger the more time you devote to practicing this skill. You will become a beacon for energy in a very short time. Many will want to take up the microphone and come through this way. Setting an appointment with Spirit for starting and ending is a good habit for advancement and balance. It is common to feel you are making it all up in the beginning but as you filter less and get confirmation from others, your confidence will increase.

Decision Chart

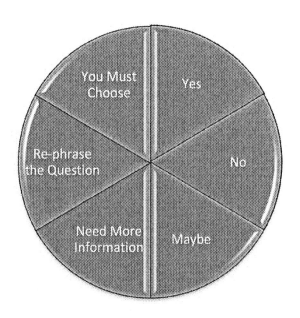

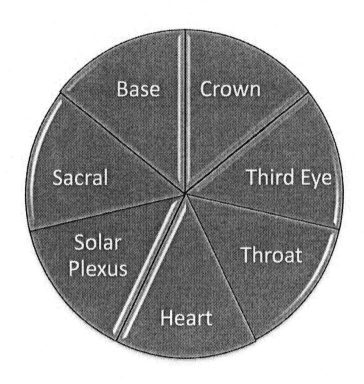

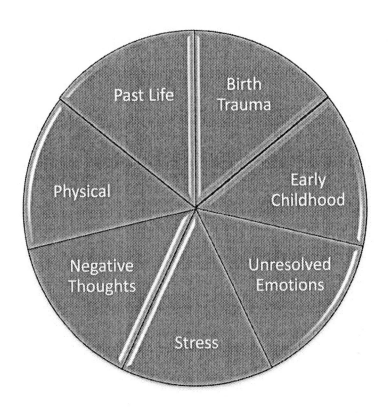

Soul Charts

There are entities of energy, of spirit, that have particular proclivities toward certain kinds of guidance and certain kinds of ways they connect with us when we are open to them. The entity that created the Soul Chart is an entity that has been asked to be called Michael. They made themselves known about 40 years ago on the Earth to a group of channelers outside of Berkeley, California. The Michael Entity is a group of about 1,050 souls who teach from what we call the causal plane – one of the dimensions that is not of the physical world. They have empathy for those of us in the physical form because they were once here.

Michael created this way of looking at our lives for us so that we could begin to bring our soul more front and center and to find our soul more tangible. The soul is who we are at our divine core. Our intellect and our ego are constantly being reflected back to us, and we're constantly getting guided and pushed and nudged in our physicality but not in the soul area. This soul chart is a way that Michael helped us in human form to be able to see something tangible, feel it, know its truth, and be able to use it as a guide for ourselves to make sure, when we look back on our day, that we are trying to bring our souls forward and are not just letting body / mind / ego run the show.

Realize that, like everything on this path to spirituality, truth has a way of taking many forms. That's why you can look at all the great religions and all the great spiritual beliefs and find that when you move away all the clutter of dogma, what is essential to the basis of spirituality, is core to all of them. They just take on different forms based on the humans who are creating them, which is the same with this. This is deep, spiritual truth, but it is not the only way to explain it. It is a great way to realize what our soul is doing here and how we can notice it and work with it in our daily lives.

Soul Age, Level, and Astuteness

When we come here, we commit to come to the physical plane for a cycle of lifetimes. There are five phases / soul ages – with seven levels to each age: the number of lifetimes you use to complete a cycle varies from soul to soul. (50-300.)

Infant is all about survival – about coming here and making it here in this very dense, slow moving body in physicality. Infant souls are very me and survival oriented – how can I stay here?

Baby is very me / you oriented. You know there is a you and you have to get along. There has to be structure and order and rules and laws in order to not have chaos. Institutions grew out of baby soul energy – government, churches, schools, etc.

Young souls are all about winning. There is a me and a you and I'm going to beat you. It is a very achievement driven, success oriented, external world driven kind of energy. This planet's culture has been very young soul, but we are moving into mature now.

Mature is about doing all the above and yet I still don't feel complete. I know there is a part of me that is bigger and more than this, and I want to touch it. You begin to go inward and immerse yourself in emotion. It is the most intense phase of the cycle. You are just wringing the juice out of every situation. It is hugely driven by relationships.

Old souls are the least on the planet. It often feels like we are not moving to the same rhythm as everyone else because we are not beating the same drum. We want to know what is next and we want to give something back to others as a legacy. Some old souls are hermit-like and have a "been there, done that" attitude.

Astute souls have a sense of springing from the soul, from the eternal nature of who they are. Most people are **non-astute** on this planet, so they don't usually go to the depth within themselves that is the connection to the All That Is. That is why so much stuff that springs from us is so judgmental, fear-based, and outcome driven. Astute souls have generally been here for three or more cycles; thus, they are most familiar with the energy of the physical plane and feel comfortable here.

Our sense of spirituality as a planet is so down. It didn't used to be that way – prior to 10,000 years ago. It's when we became a civilization that we seemed to have lost it. Our quest for life at any cost has cast a fear over the dying process. Humans are at a real pivotal point, and it is no accident that we are here now.

Role

This overleaf is the only one you keep through the whole cycle. It's the energy you emit as your anchor. Each overleaf has a positive and negative aspect. You need to watch that because when you are coming from the positive pole that is your soul, your spiritual essence. When you are coming from the negative pole, it is your ego running the show.

Your **Essence Twin** is a soul relationship that is the strongest because you come into each lifetime (to some degree) and agree to be mirrors for each other and to support and challenge and push and nudge and love and do whatever is required to be the mirror to help you grow and move forward, so it can be a very prickly relationship. Because you have been together for so many lifetimes this cycle, your roles have a bleed-through effect on each other.

Goal and Mode

The goal is to show up in your life continually so you feel like you are mastering it. The mode is the way to achieve the goal. They are like the hand and the glove. You just need to watch the negative pole of both of those.

Attitude

Attitude is your attitude toward life. We do all seven of these, but there is one that when we are under stress especially or when we just need to go deep, we react with this attitude.

Chief Feature

This is the only one of the seven that you did not emerge from your mother's womb with. This one develops after you get here through your upbringing, your imprinting from your family, and the culture you are in. By the time you are a teenager, you develop it. When we get into our 30s, we tend to not rely on the chief feature as much as when we are younger. We use it to learn over and over again.

Centering

As a soul, we come into the physical plane knowing we need to center ourselves; that we are going to need balance. We are going to get bombarded with so much distraction and ego stuff to cover our soul that we come programmed to know in what way we are going to find our center – how we are going to balance as we interact with the world. All of us do all three things.

An example – if you were sitting in the window of a restaurant and a car accident happened, the intellectually centered soul would first say, "Oh the black car came around the corner and the red car didn't stop." The emotionally centered souls would not think of the cars. They would see kids and blood and feel what just happened for those people. The moving center soul is out the door, calling 911, and pulling people out of the car before he or she thought or felt what happened. This is important in getting along with people because you have to be cognizant of from where the others are centering.

Body Type

We choose it as the soul we are. Certain roles like certain body types. For example, **Jupiter** is one of the most magnanimous, expansive types – willing to take in everyone and help. Servers love Jupiter for this reason. Kings love Jupiter because it makes their presence known. They can't melt into the woodwork. You cannot miss a Jupiter.

You can just put your chart away in a drawer or you can put it someplace where you will look at it occasionally so that you keep being reminded of your soul's traits. You put off a different energy when you reflect and are able to point to the soulful events in your day. That's what adds to the energy and ultimately brings it to the place it needs to be. It is your recognition and your realization in the conscious world that you are a soul and that your soul is impacting on what your day is all about. That is the true value of the soul overleaf chart. This is also a good starting point to understand others, if you create a chart when working with a new client. For example, an overwhelmed Server would not be told to "stop" serving others but would be helped to discern their own boundary of service and bondage.

I recommend *The Michael Handbook: A channeled System for Self Understanding* by Jose Stevens and Simon Warwick-Smith and *Michael: The Basic Teachings* by Aaron Christeaan, J.P. Van Hulle and M.C. Clark for additional explanations on the Soul Overleaf Chart.

Soul Overleaf Chart

Name:	Soul Age:		Level:		Cycle:		Astute:
	EXPRESSION		**INSPIRATION**		**ACTION**		**ASSINIATION**
	Ordinal	Exalted	Ordinal	Exalted	Ordinal	Exalted	Neutral
Role	+Creation **Artisan** -Self Deception	Dissemination **Sage** -Verbosity	+Service **Server** -Bondage	+Compassion **Priest** - Zeal	+Persuasion **Warrior** -Intimidation	+Mastery **King** -Tyranny	+Knowledge **Scholar** -Theory
Goal	+Sophistication **Discrimination** -Rejection	+Agape **Acceptance** -Ingratiation	+Simplicity **Re-Evaluation** -Withdrawal	+Evolution **Growth** -Confusion	+Devotion **Submission** -Exploited	+Leadership **Dominance** -Dictatorship	+Free Flowing **Stagnation/Relaxation** -Inertia
Mode	+Deliberation **Caution** -Phobia	+Authority **Power** -Oppression	+Restraint **Repression** -Inhibition	+Self-Actualization **Passion** -Identification	+Persistence **Perseverance** -Unchanging	+Vigor **Aggression** -Belligerence	+Clarity **Observation** -Surveillance
Attitude	+Investigative **Skeptic** -Suspicion	+Coalescence **Idealist** -Naiveté	+Tranquility **Stoic** -Resignation	+Verification **Spiritualist** -Beliefs	+Contradiction **Cynic** -Scorn	+Objective **Realist** -Subjective	+Practical **Pragmatist** -Dogmatic
Chief Feature	+Sacrifice **Self-Defeat** -Suicidal	+Appetite **Greed** -Insatiability	+Humility **Self-Depreciation** -Abasement	+Pride **Arrogance** -Vanity	+Selflessness **Martyr** -Victimization	+Daring **Impatience** -Intolerance	+Determination **Stubbornness** -Obstinacy
Center	+Insight **Intellectual** -Reasoning		+Perception **Emotional** -Sentimentality		+Productive **Moving** -Frenetic		
Body Types 1 & 2	+Grandeur **Jupiter** -Overwhelming	+Agile **Mercury** -Nervous	+Luminous **Lunar** -Pallid	+Rugged **Saturn** -Gaunt	+Voluptuous **Venus** -Sloppy	+Wiry **Mars** -Impulsive	+Radiant **Solar** -Ethereal

Levels and Cycles

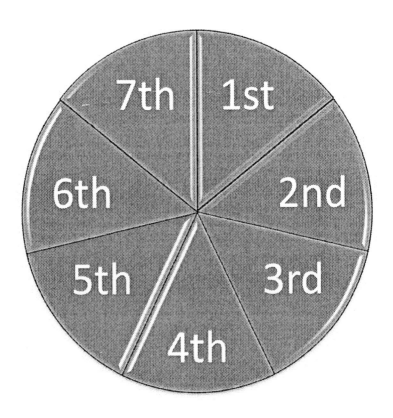

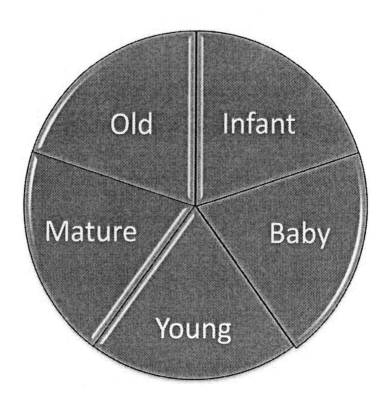

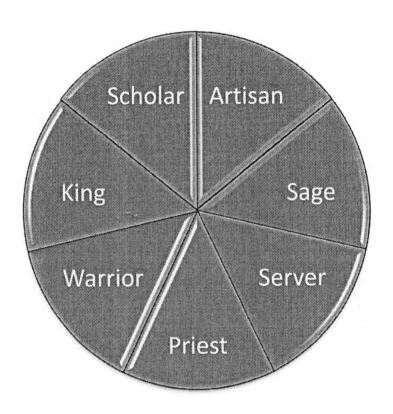

Goals

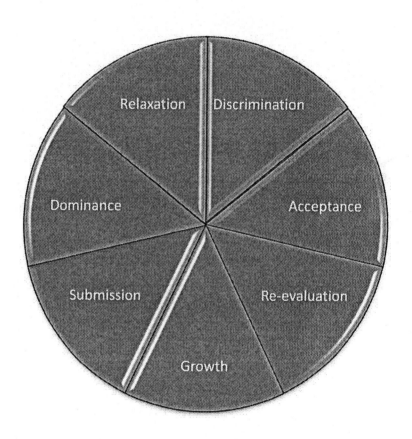

Mode

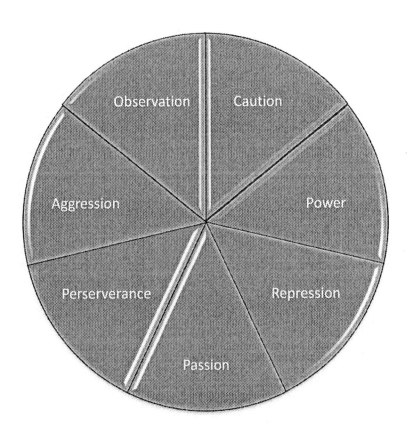

Attitude

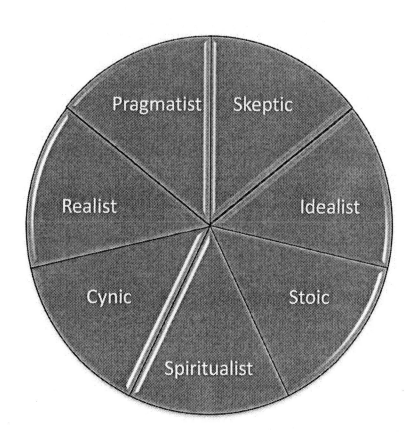

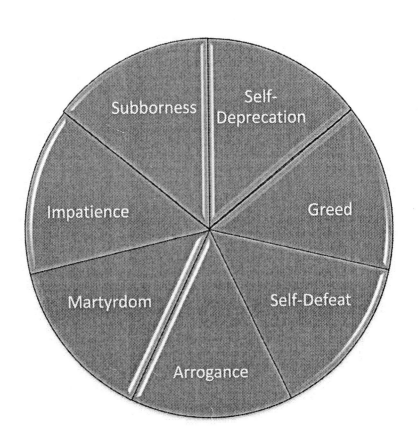

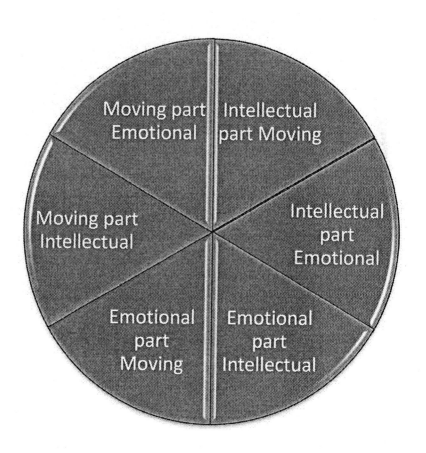

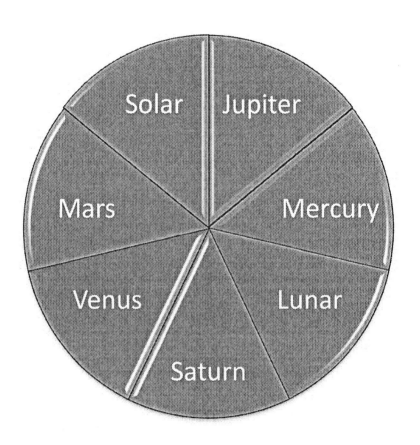

Acknowledgements

Thanks to My Writing Support Group

Mike Somers

Lydia Marie Marino

Bryan Hayes

Holly DelQuadri

Daphne Lewis

Dana Sanchez

Cathy Silver

Sally Baldwin

Rose Hunt

Trish Joyce

Tiffany Ardizzone

Craig Rosenblatt

About the Author

Wendy Sloan

Wendy Sloan is a Holistic Healer who helps individuals make the transition from surviving to thriving using the tools of Hypnosis, Massage Therapy, Reiki, Channeling, and Coaching. An author and international speaker, Wendy started her business in 2000 to help others manage change and reduce stress while enjoying the moment. Prior to this, Wendy was a grocery store manager and supervised over 170 employees. She has traveled to India, Brazil, Europe, North Africa, Austrailia, and to all 50 of the United States. Wendy has a BS degree in Psychology from Nova Southeastern University and an MBA degree from Florida Atlantic University. She is the director of The Synergy Central and currently offers a wide range of programs and services including individual or group sessions, seminars, and keynote speeches.

Please visit www.theloveenergythread.com

or email Wendy at

wendysloan2015@yahoo.com

139